PIES, GLORIOUS PIES

PIES, GLORIOUS PIES

Brilliant recipes for mouth-wateringly tasty pies

Maxine Clark

photography by Steve Painter

rps

LONDON • NEW YORK

Dedicated to the memory of Norman Lee (1927–2012), artist, raconteur, *bon viveur* and a man who loved a Scotch 'peh'.

Maxine Clark is a leading food stylist and cookery writer, as well as a gifted teacher. She gained a Distinction when training at Leiths School of Food and Wine in London, and became a teacher there after graduating. Maxine has been teaching gourmet cookery holidays in Italy for more than 20 years. Maxine is a teaching fellow in Food and Consumer Sciences at The University of Abertay, Dundee and also acts as a development chef. Her work appears regularly in popular magazines, including *BBC Good Food* and *Food and Travel*.

Steve Painter worked for Ryland Peters & Small for ten years, designing, art directing photography and prop styling many of their books, including the bestselling *The Hummingbird Bakery Cookbook*. Now freelance, he lives in the seaside town of Hastings, where he designed and photographed this book. For Ryland Peters & Small he has also photographed *How To Make Bread*, *Meg Rivers Home Baking* and *Gelato*.

DESIGN, PHOTOGRAPHY AND PROP STYLING Steve Painter
EDITOR Rebecca Woods
PRODUCTION MANAGER Gordana Simakovic
ART DIRECTOR Leslie Harrington
EDITORIAL DIRECTOR Julia Charles

INDEXER Hilary Bird
FOOD STYLIST Lucy McKelvie
FOOD STYLIST'S ASSISTANT Ellie Jarvis

First published in 2012 by
Ryland Peters & Small
20–21 Jockey's Fields
London WC1R 4BW
and
519 Broadway, 5th Floor
New York, NY 10012
www.rylandpeters.com

10 9 8 7 6 5 4 3 2 1

Text © Maxine Clark 2012
Design and photographs
© Ryland Peters & Small 2012

Printed in China

ISBN: 978-1-84975-261-9

A CIP record for this book is available from the British Library.

US Library of Congress CIP data has been applied for.

NOTES
• All spoon measurements are level unless otherwise specified.

• All vegetables are medium sized unless otherwise specified.

• All eggs are medium (UK) or large (US), unless otherwise specified. It is recommended that free-range, organic eggs be used whenever possible.

• Ovens should be preheated to the specified temperatures. We recommend using an oven thermometer. If using a fan-assisted oven, adjust temperatures according to the manufacturer's instructions.

CONTENTS

INTRODUCTION

I simply can't remember life without a pie. Not that I was weaned on pies, but pies were, and still are, very much part of life here in Scotland where I was born and now live. There's something truly comforting and comfortable about a pie – a secret filling nestling inside a golden crust. Watch someone bite into a pie and they will inevitably make some sort of pleasing facial gesture and look at the pie they have just bitten into to examine its glorious contents!

Of course there are a million different pies out in the big wide world – single-crust, double-crust, raised, cold, hot, small, large, with potato topping instead of pastry. Every country has their own variations of a pastry-enclosed filling, be it an Indian samosa, an Italian torta, a Spanish or Mexican empanada, a Scotch bridie, an English steak and kidney pie with mash and liquor, or an American pot or plate pie.

My first memories of pies were the little rhubarb pies sitting in ranks in the baker's window that I passed every day on my way home from school. The pastry was a hot-water crust and the filling quite tart, but they were dusted in a thick coating of sugar and I would buy one and munch it on the bus, showering sugar all over my uniform! Then there was my mum's apple pie: single crust and baked in her grandmother's round enamel dish, with a crackling sugary crust on top. And my brother and sister and I just couldn't wait to have our Fray Bentos Steak and Kidney Pie – we thought that a pie in a can was the height of chic!

Since then my tastes have broadened somewhat. Cornish holidays in the late 60s were a pie eye-opener, from Elizabeth Brown's insanely deep and delicious apple pie, served in the restaurant of the St Mawes Hotel, to Doris Tiddy's legendary pasties (see page 92). After tasting these, there was no going back. I realized the beauty and diversity of a well-made pastry crust and just how delicious a filling could be – however simple the ingredients! Then at Leiths School of Food and Wine came the revelation of executing a hot-water crust and 'raising' a pie – well there was now no going back, and pies became an essential part of life.

Why? I think it's really the pastry. I love it and love making it in all its diverse forms. I took a while to master it, but once it clicked a whole new world of possibilities opened up. So follow my hints and tips learned and gathered over years of pastry making and you simply won't go wrong. From Basic Shortcrust or Suet Crust, to French Rich Butter Pastry, they all have their purposes and functions. Some make a better top crust than others, some are meant to stand upright and encase a filling whereas others are designed to puff up and melt in the mouth. All these pastries are made by mixing flour with either only butter or a mix of butter and lard or olive oil or suet. Each has a different flavour and texture, depending on the fat and flour used or the pastry method followed, to perfectly complement the filling hidden inside.

You can bake almost anything in a pie – from four and twenty blackbirds to unfortunate barber-shop customers. All will taste the better for a pastry crust. The secret with pies is not to make the filling too wet or it will ooze out of the pastry and make it go soggy before it has time to crisp up (and I have a good 'waterproofing' technique using egg wash to prevent this). Take a look at Pie Practicalities (see page 13) and Equipment (see page 9) before you start for tips on achieving perfect pies for every occasion.

The book is divided simply into four chapters: Everyday Pies, Posh Pies, Portable Pies and Sweet Pies. Some are very easy, others require a little more skill and patience, and other more complicated pies just require careful time-planning.

I have enjoyed writing this book immensely, and it is so satisfying to see a lot of old friends appearing between the pages. I hope you find inspiration here to bake a pie or two… and did I say that they make very, very welcome gifts? Eyes will light up!

EQUIPMENT

For making everyday pies, no special equipment is necessary except the basics: a cool work surface, kitchen scales and a bowl for making pastry, plus a pie plate, rolling pin, sharp knife, baking 'beans', clingfilm/plastic wrap and maybe a pastry brush. However, if you become a serious pie-maker and bake pies regularly, you may like to invest in a special mould or pan, a wooden pie dolly for individual raised pies, pie funnels, pastry cutters and a lattice roller or pastry wheel

FOR PASTRY-MAKING

A large cool work surface (a marble slab if you are lucky, but make sure it is big enough) is essential for making a pie. Never roll out pastry in a cramped area or you will risk rolling unevenly or stretching the pastry. The surface should be cool (not next to the hob/stove or over a fridge) to prevent the pastry becoming soft and unmanageable.

Accurate weighing scales or measuring cups to get the quantities and proportions correct.

Measuring spoons for the accurate measuring necessary with all baking. Recipes in this book require all measurements to be level.

Large and small heatproof measuring jugs/pitchers. These are dual purpose – for accurate measuring of liquid ingredients, and suitability for the microwave.

Fine and medium sieves/strainers are essential for sifting all flour to aerate it and remove any lumps, leading to a lighter pastry. Icing/confectioners' sugar should always be sifted in a fine sieve/strainer – any lumps will never beat out.

Assorted mixing bowls – I find I use light plastic bowls or wide stainless steel ones for pastry-making, but ceramic or Pyrex are perfectly suitable. The important thing is to make sure the bowl is big enough for the job – you want plenty of room to move your hands and the ingredients when rubbing in. This, too, aerates the pastry.

A food processor is a *must* if you have hot hands, or if you think you can't make pastry! It removes the fear of butter melting into the flour, because it mixes fat and flour so quickly and evenly. Just remember to pulse the machine when adding liquids so that the

dough will not be overworked and become tough.

A flour sifter/shaker is not absolutely necessary, but it does stop you adding too much extra flour to the work surface or pastry. Too much flour destroys the proportions and affects taste and texture.

Several pastry brushes so that you always have a dry one to hand for brushing excess flour off pastry, and one for brushing on liquids and glazes.

A pastry/dough scraper for scraping the dough off a work surface, and for cleaning off all the messy bits. Indispensable.

A palette knife can be substituted for a pastry scraper, but is best used for chopping in the flour in French pastries such as French Butter Pie Pastry (see page 29).

Microplane graters were a revelation to me, and once acquired, you'll wonder how you ever lived without them. There are three essential grades – fine, medium and coarse. Fine is perfect for grating lemons, nutmeg, garlic, ginger and Parmesan. A medium grain is good for other cheeses and general grating, while coarse is perfect for grating shards of butter into pastry, such as for Cheat's Puff Pastry (see page 27).

A pastry blender is something I have used only occasionally, but some cooks swear by it. It is a series of thin metal loops connected to a handle, which you use to cut the fat into the flour. It prevents 'hot hand syndrome' and aerates the pastry. I prefer an old round-bladed cutlery knife (or two – one in each hand) to cut in the fat.

All-purpose clingfilm/plastic wrap or plastic bags are absolutely necessary to wrap pastry before chilling or freezing, protecting it and preventing it from drying out.

Baking beans are essential for weighting down the pastry once the pan is lined. They will stop the pastry collapsing as it cooks when baking blind. Although you can buy smart ceramic baking beans, I prefer to use dried beans, rice, lentils and pasta or a mix of all of them – they can be used over and over again, and cost next to nothing.

A bottle of ice-cold water should always be in the fridge before you start, so that you will have chilled water to hand for pastry-making.

CHOOSING PIE PLATES AND PANS

Note: I do not use non-stick or silicone bakeware for pie-making – I find that the pastry 'sweats' and never crisps up sufficiently. Likewise, I do not cook pastry in Pyrex or ceramic dishes for the same reason – they do not conduct the heat as well as metal does and so the pastry just doesn't cook properly.

Metal or enamel pie plates with a rim to take a good crust – both deep and shallow – are essential for tarts that need a decorative edge. Traditional British pie plates are made of enamel, the inside is gently rounded and the lip is quite wide (about 2.5 cm/ 1 inch). American pie plates tend to be deeper with a narrower lip and are usually made of enamel or metal.

Assorted round springform pans are great for deeper pies as they are easy to remove once cooked.

Individual pie dishes come in various shapes and sizes and are often made from traditional glazed pottery. The deep ones are perfect for a top-crust pie with a generous filling.

Metal loaf pans make pies that can be portioned very neatly. They make a good substitute for the fancy raised pie moulds, which are pricey and hard to find.

Traditional raised pie moulds make pies look fabulous if you can get hold of them. They are hinged or cleverly clip together.

Bun, patty or even muffin pans are wonderful for making small pies in bulk – look for ones with straight sides (mini Victoria sponge pans).

With the current pie-loving trend, new pie pans are appearing all the time – keep an eye open in your local cookshop. However, many pans or moulds can be adapted to cooking pies – just think creatively!

ROLLING OUT, LINING AND SHAPING

Long straight rolling pin (wooden or nylon) with no handles. (I find that handles spoil the even rolling action of the pin.) Always keep your rolling pin somewhere where the surface won't be damaged by other kitchen utensils (i.e. not in the utensil drawer!)

Sharp cook's knife or thin-bladed filleting knife for trimming – it must be razor-sharp to cut through the pastry and not drag it.

Large serrated knife for trimming and slicing – this stays nice and sharp and is good for cutting baked pie crusts.

A fork for pricking bases and decorating.

Assorted sizes of palette knife – a large one will help to loosen rolled-out pastry from a work surface, a small one will lift little pastry circles into a tart pan and a tiny one will lift decorations onto the tart edge.

A pie dolly is useful if you are a serious raised pie-maker! However, any cylindrical object (such as a jam jar, pot, can etc.) can be used instead.

Clingfilm/plastic wrap, kitchen foil and non-stick baking parchment are indispensible for wrapping pastry, lining pans and baking blind. You can also roll pastry directly onto non-stick baking parchment, then you can lift it up and place it over the pan without fear of stretching it. It can help keep the shape of a hand-raised pie while it cooks when tied firmly around the middle with a piece of string.

DECORATING PASTRY

Pastry cutters of all types are great for customizing your pies and tarts. Try leaf or animal cutters to create decorative edges and tops.

Pastry wheels make short work of cutting straight lines and give pretty decorative edges.

A small sharp knife will help to cut patterns on decorations.

Forks of varying sizes for marking edges.

A metal ruler helps mark out pastry for cutting.

Thick cardboard and a craft knife for making your own templates for pastry decorations.

A lattice roller can make a professional-looking lattice top for pies. It acts like a roller, cutting out a lattice, which is then opened up like a web to drape over a tart. It lacks the homemade look, however!

BAKING AND COOLING PIES

An electronic timer is one of my most essential pieces of kit. You cannot possibly cook pastry and not burn it without one!

Oven gloves are a must; no damp dish towels to burn your hands!

Heavy baking sheet – important to put one into the oven as it preheats, especially if not baking blind, as it will help conduct the heat through the base of the pan and cook the pastry.

Large fish slice/spatula or cake-lifter (like a small baking sheet with a handle) will help to lift the pie or tart onto a plate without it falling to bits.

Wire or metal cooling racks in assorted sizes.

Serrated palette knife is useful to slice the pie or tart then serve it or lift onto a plate.

PIE PRACTICALITIES

For perfect results every time, follow these simple yet effective tips garnered from a lifetime of pastry and pie making. I only wish someone had told me these when I began to make pastry – they would have prevented my initial disasters and spared me a lot of frustration! I have hot hands, and using the food processor changed the way I make pastry forever! It cannot be emphasized enough that pastry likes a cool environment and not too much handling. Read on and digest and you will become a master pieman/woman!

• When making pastry, water/liquid quantities are never exact as there are so many variables. A good rule of thumb is to add slightly less than is stated, as you can always add more, but too much and the dough is lost!

• There is no need to grease a pan before lining. All pastry has fat in it and will, in effect, be non-stick. It is the filling leaking out over the edges or through holes that makes pastry stick, so make sure the pastry is completely sealed.

• If in doubt, chill, chill, chill! Raw pastry will benefit from thorough chilling at every stage – I like to freeze pastry-lined pans before baking blind as this really sets the pastry, therefore holding its shape. Freeze the unbaked pie crust after lining the pan with pastry – even 15 minutes will do (you can keep the uncooked pie crust frozen and wrapped for up to 3 months). This gives the pastry a good rest and makes the pie or tart easy to line with kitchen foil or clingfilm/plastic wrap and baking beans when baking blind. Work quickly and pop it into the oven before it thaws, and you will have a perfect pie crust!

• Use a rolling pin to lift a pastry lid over the pie to prevent stretching the pastry.

• Always chill a double-crust pie before baking.

• Always glaze then chill a pie before making any marks on the pastry – it will be easier to do and the pattern will remain distinct.

• Always chill a pie before making slits in the pastry – making the slits will be easier.

• Always place a pie on a baking sheet before baking (use a cake-lifter to slide it in and out of the oven). This will make it easier to lift and prevent any spillage burning on the bottom of the oven.

• Casserole-style fillings can be made in advance and stored in the fridge for a couple of days, or even frozen. Not only is this added convenience, but it also allows the flavours in the filling time to develop.

• To avoid a soggy pie bottom, make sure cooked fillings are completely cold when filling the pie. To be absolutely sure, when baking blind, brush the base of the pie with beaten egg after removing the baking beans and returning to the oven to dry off. This will create a 'waterproof' base. My mother always spread 2 tablespoons semolina flour mixed with sugar over the base of her apple pie to absorb cooking juices and prevent 'soggy bottom' – this was learned from watching her grandmother, a professional baker.

• To glaze the sides of a pie baked in a mould or pan with sides: once cooked, remove it from the oven and allow to rest for 10 minutes, remove the sides, brush with milk or beaten egg and return to the oven to set the glaze. Cover the top of the pie with kitchen foil to prevent it becoming darker than the sides.

• I usually set fan ovens 20 degrees lower than regular convection ovens as they tend to run very hot. Consult the manufacturer's handbook. This is very important when baking.

TECHNIQUES

ROLLING THE PASTRY

• Pastry is easier to roll out if shaped into a ball, then flattened to a thick disk **(1)** before wrapping and chilling. Make sure you allow the pastry to soften slightly before rolling.

• Lightly dust a work surface with flour.

• To prevent sticking, flour your hands and the rolling pin rather than showering the pastry with extra flour – this will avoid a build-up of powdery flour on the pastry.

• When rolling pastry, keep it moving on a 'hovercraft' of flour and it will never stick. Or try rolling pastry directly onto a piece of non-stick baking parchment or clingfilm/plastic wrap – this allows it be moved around easily and it will not stick to the work surface. The pastry can also be easily lifted and laid over a pie or tart without it stretching.

• Hold the rolling pin at either end, place on the pastry dough and always roll directly away from you. Move the pastry around by short turns in one direction so that you roll it evenly **(2)**. Never flip the pastry over.

• Keep the rolling pin level for even thickness. Setting two chopsticks (or similar) on either side of the dough before rolling will help you to roll it out evenly to the thickness of the chopstick.

• Place your pie pan or dish on top of the rolled-out pastry to check it is large enough to cover the surface **(3)**. Don't forget to include the height of the sides in your calculations.

• Once the pastry is the right size and thickness, roll the flour-dusted pastry around the rolling pin to help you to pick it up **(4)** – this will avoid stretching the pastry and stop it shrinking when cooking.

1   2   3   4

LINING A PIE PAN OR DISH

• Drape the pastry over the pan and work it into the corners, being careful not to tear the pastry **(5)**. (There is no need to grease a pie pan before lining, unless you have a vertical surface that you want the pastry to adhere to i.e. a deep loaf pan.)

• Use a small piece of extra pastry wrapped in a piece of clingfilm/plastic wrap to help to push the pastry into the edges of the pan **(6)**.

• To make a single-crust pie, press the pastry up the sides of the pan and cut off the overhang with a very sharp knife. Or use a rolling pin to roll over the top **(7)**, which will trim off any excess pastry very neatly **(8)**. (Don't cut trim the excess if making a double-crust pie – you will trim both crusts off together.) Chill or freeze before baking.

BAKING BLIND

By 'baking blind', you pre-cook the pie crust so that it cooks through before the filling goes in and is less likely to become soggy. It also stops the pastry edges from collapsing into the filling.

• Prick the pie crust all over with a fork **(9)**.

• Line the pie crust with a piece of well-crumpled baking parchment or kitchen foil and fill with a layer of baking beans **(10)**.

• Bake the pastry at 200°C (400°F) Gas 6 for 15 minutes then remove from the oven and lift out the baking parchment or foil and baking beans **(11)**. Return to the oven and bake for a further 10 minutes or so until dried out, lightly golden and cooked through **(12)**. Leave to cool.

FILLING THE PIE

• Once the pan is lined, spoon in the cold filling, being careful not to splash the edges or overfill so that the top will seal properly.

• If the filling is likely to collapse slightly as it cooks (this will happen if raw fruit or meat is put in the pie), insert a pie funnel before you add the pastry lid. This will help steam escape as well as holding the pastry up so it cooks evenly and doesn't collapse into the dish. This is particularly important when putting a single-crust lid onto a deep-dish pie – the pastry can easily slip off the edges and collapse into the filling.

• Cover and cook as soon as possible.

TO MAKE A SINGLE-CRUST DEEP-DISH PIE

• Roll out the pastry evenly on a lightly floured surface. Use the inverted dish as a guide to measure an extra 5 cm/2 inches all the way around the dish.

• With a small sharp knife, cut a 2.5-cm/1-inch strip of pastry from the edge, following the shape of the pie dish (1).

• Upturn the pie dish and, using a pastry brush, moisten the edge or rim of the dish with a little water (2). Take the 2.5-cm/1-inch strip of pastry, lay it around the rim of the dish and gently press onto the rim (3). Brush the strip with a little water (4).

• If using, place a pie funnel in the centre of the dish. Spoon the filling into the dish, mounding it up in the middle of the pie (and around the pie funnel, if using), so that when the pastry lid goes on, it will sit lightly on top of the filling.

• Loosely roll the pastry lid over the rolling pin, then lift up over the pie dish and unroll the pastry so that it falls into position over the dish, centring it as much as possible (5). (If using a pie funnel,

pre-cut a slash or hole in the centre of the pastry so that this falls over the funnel when the pastry lid is lifted on top.)

• Press the edge of the pastry lid down onto the dampened rim of pastry, pressing firmly to seal.

• Trim any excess pastry away from the edges with a sharp knife, holding the knife at an angle away from the pie dish (6). If not using a pie funnel, cut a slit or small hole in the top of the pastry to allow the steam to escape during cooking.

• 'Knocking-up' separates the layers in puff pastry, which helps it rise. It also seals the base and lid pastry together (in both puff and shortcrust) so that they do not come apart during cooking and allow the filling to leak. Hold a knife horizontally and use the sharp edge to tap the edge of the pastry all the way around the dish (7).

• Use the tines of a floured fork to press down on the rim of the pastry for a decorative finish (8) (for alternatives, see page 20) and decorate with pastry trimmings if wished, then glaze (see page 21).

TO MAKE A DOUBLE-CRUST PIE

• First divide the pastry into two pieces, one slightly bigger than the other.

• Take the larger piece of pastry and roll it out on a lightly floured surface to a size that is 2.5 cm/1 inch wider than the inverted pie plate or pan.

• Loosely roll the pastry over the rolling pin, then lift up over the pie plate and unroll the pastry so that it falls into position over the plate, centring it as much as possible (1).

• Ease the pastry into the bottom of the plate by lifting it upwards and then gently lowering it into position. Press down into place with your fingertips along the base and sides of the dish. Wrap a piece of extra pastry in clingfilm/plastic wrap and use this to gently press the pastry into the pan (2).

• Using a sharp knife trim, off any excess pastry from the rim of the pan (3).

• Spoon in the filling, mounding it up in the middle of the pie. Clean the rim if splashed.

• Using a pastry brush, moisten the edge or rim of the dish with a little water.

• Roll out the smaller piece of pastry so that it is about 2.5 cm/1 inch bigger than the rim of the pan. Lift it up with the rolling pin as before and unroll it over the top of the pan (4). There are two ways to seal the edges together:

• Press the two edges together (5) and trim off excess pastry (6), then crimp (7) to firmly seal and decorate the edge. Chill for at least 20 minutes before baking.

OR

• Press the two edges together and trim off the excess pastry but leave 1.25 cm/½ inch hanging over the side. Fold the pastry overhang neatly under the rim of the pan and press the edges together again, making sure that the pie is fully sealed. Crimp and decorate the edge. Chill for at least 20 minutes before baking.

• Finally, cut two slits in the top of the pie (8), then glaze (see page 21) and chill before decorating with pastry trimmings.

ADDING A DECORATIVE EDGE OR TOP

There are countless ways of decorating pastry edges on a pie – many designs are steeped in tradition and specifically used for particular pies or tarts. The simplest is the forked edge, followed by using the tip of a knife to create cuts and folds. The edge is normally brushed with milk or beaten egg to give a soft sheen or shiny glaze, then the pie is chilled to set the pastry before baking.

Crimped or scalloped edge

Push one index finger downwards against the outside edge of the rim. With your index finger and thumb of the other hand, pinch it to form a sort of ruffle. Repeat around the entire edge, leaving a slight space between each ruffle. Alternatively, scallop the edge by pressing your thumb firmly down on top of the pastry border and drawing the back of a knife inwards and slightly upwards against your thumb. Continue all the way around to scallop the entire edge.

Rope edge

Press your thumb into the pastry edge at an angle. Then pinch the pastry between your thumb and the knuckle of your index finger. Place your thumb in the indentation left by your index finger. Pinch as before and repeat around the entire edge.

Fork edge

The edge of the pastry is marked by pressing the tines of a fork flat across the surface, so that the marks radiate outwards. Press quite hard to make deep indentations.

Dog edge

These cuts look rather like a dog's floppy ears, hence the name! Using a sharp knife, make small cuts the width of the pastry edge about a thumb's breadth apart. Fold every alternate 'ear' over towards the centre of the pan or dish and press the edge (not the fold) to seal.

Devil edge

I call this design 'devil edge' because I think it looks jaggedly devilish! It is the traditional edge for a treacle tart. Using a sharp knife, make small cuts the width of the pastry edge about a thumb's breadth apart. Fold over every 'flap' diagonally onto itself towards the centre of the pan or dish, pressing the tips (not the folds) downwards to seal.

Classic lattice

The lattice top gives a pretty decorative finish to a pie or tart, teasingly half-concealing what lies beneath. There are many ways of doing this by hand – you can simply arrange the strips over each other, interweave them or twist them to give a barley-sugar effect. If this looks too fiddly and time-consuming, use a lattice roller to create a lovely lacy effect. If there is no pastry rim, set a ring of pastry around the edge of the filled tart to keep the strips in place.

To make a lattice by hand: roll out the pastry thinly. Decide how many strips will fit across the pie. Cut into equal strips with the knife, using a ruler as a guide. If there is no rim or it is not wide enough to support the lattice, cut out a ring of pastry to fit inside the edge of the pie. Dampen the edge, then start arranging the strips at equal intervals across the filled pie. If you are not sure about where to position the strips, lay them halfway across at first, folding them back so that they can be easily moved if necessary. Place a second set of strips across the first, either interweaving them like basketwork, or simply setting them at right angles to the first strips. Trim the edges of the strips for a neat finish.

To make a lattice with a lattice roller: roll out the pastry to a size slightly larger than the pie. Roll the cutter the length of the pastry, pressing firmly to make clean cuts. Gently pull the lattice open and drape over a rolling pin. Lift carefully onto the pie, opening the mesh evenly. Press firmly around the edges to seal, trim off the excess pastry and finish with a decorative edge.

DECORATING THE PIE

You can decorate a pie by cutting out shapes from the remaining pastry trimmings – or make a little extra just to decorate. I collect cutters from my trips abroad just for this purpose! The vintage or antique ones are the best – clean shapes and beautifully made. I have my great-grandmother's and will not let them out of my sight!

Decorating a pie using pastry cutters

Use a shaped pastry cutter to cut out the chosen shape, teasing away any excess pastry if necessary. Brush the top of the pie with glaze where you want the decoration to sit. Gently lift up your shape (a palette knife is good for this) and place onto the pie, pressing down gently. Brush a little more glaze over the top of the decoration.

Decorating a pie using stencils

For a more personal design, you can create your own stencils for the decoration. Draw or trace your design onto a piece of card and cut out with a craft knife. Roll out the pastry to 2 mm/$\frac{1}{16}$ inch thick and place the stencil on top. Use the tip of a small sharp knife to draw around the stencil through the pastry. Remove the stencil and tease away the excess pastry, leaving your shape. Brush the pie with glaze or water and, using a palette knife, lift the pastry cut-out onto the pie. Press lightly to attach, then brush with glaze.

GLAZING THE PIE

The tops of pies are usually glazed to give a golden, shiny finish that tempts the eye! A glaze will also seal the surface and helps give the pie a longer life. Adding salt to a glaze will give the finished glaze a darker colour.

Pastry glazes

• Whole egg beaten with salt.
• Lightly beaten egg yolk and salt for the shiniest finish (strain through a tea strainer before using).
• Lightly beaten egg white and sugar for a pale bubbly crunchy crust.
• Whole milk will help the pastry go pale golden but not so shiny (usually used on shortcrust pastry).
• Cream mixed with milk will give a shiny glaze (usually used on shortcrust pastry).

Brush the glaze evenly over the surface of the pie. Try not to get any glaze on the pan or the pie will stick to it. If you are using a pastry that will rise (i.e. puff pastry), be careful not to brush the glaze over the edges as it will glue the layers together and stop it rising. Chill to set, then brush again just before baking. Adding a second coat of glaze 10 minutes towards the end of baking will give a fabulous shiny golden finish.

BASIC SHORTCRUST PASTRY

This is the classic method for making short and crumbly shortcrust pastry. It is made with half butter and half lard – the butter for colour and flavour and the lard for shortness. If you have cool hands, the hand method is best as it will incorporate more air than in a food processor. If you have hot hands, the food processor is a blessing! The quantities of water added vary according to the humidity of the flour. Always add less than it says – you can always add more if it is dry, but once it is a sticky mess, it could prove disastrous!

250 g/2 cups plain/
all-purpose flour

a pinch of salt

50 g/3 tablespoons lard (or white cooking fat/shortening), chilled and diced

75 g/5 tablespoons unsalted butter, chilled and diced

2–3 tablespoons ice-cold water

MAKES ABOUT 400 G/14 OZ.
(ENOUGH TO LINE THE BASE OF A
23–25-CM/9–10-INCH LOOSE-BASED
TART PAN OR MAKE A DOUBLE CRUST
FOR A 20–23-CM/8–9-INCH PIE PLATE)

THE CLASSIC WAY

Sift the flour and salt together into a large mixing bowl (1).

Add the lard and butter (2) and rub in (3) until the mixture resembles breadcrumbs (4). Add enough of the water (5) to bring the pastry together, and stir in (6).

Tip onto a lightly floured surface (7) and knead lightly to bring the dough together (8). Shape into a flattened ball, wrap in clingfilm/plastic wrap and chill for at least 30 minutes before rolling out and using in the recipe.

TIP: To make a vegan variation, simply substitute 125 g/4½ oz. vegan margarine for the lard and butter in the recipe and follow the method as above.

1   2   3   4

THE FOOD PROCESSOR METHOD

Sift the flour and salt together into the bowl of the machine. Add the lard and butter (9) and process for about 30 seconds until the mixture resembles fine breadcrumbs (10). Pour in 2 tablespoons of the water (11) and pulse for 10 seconds. The dough should start to come together in large raggy lumps (12). If not, add another tablespoon of water and pulse again. As soon as the dough forms one big lump (don't overprocess or the pastry will be tough), tip out onto a lightly floured surface and knead lightly. Shape into a flattened ball, wrap in clingfilm/plastic wrap and chill for at least 30 minutes before rolling out and using in the recipe.

RICH SHORTCRUST PASTRY

This is a wonderfully light and crumbly pastry, but enriched with egg and made with butter only. It is best for richer pies and tarts, or where the taste of the pastry is very important – not just a carrier for the filling.

250 g/2 cups plain/
all-purpose flour

½ teaspoon salt

125 g/1 stick unsalted butter,
chilled and diced

2 egg yolks

2–3 tablespoons ice-cold water

MAKES ABOUT 400 G/14 OZ. (ENOUGH TO LINE THE BASE OF A 23-25-CM/9-10-INCH FLUTED TART PAN OR TO MAKE A DOUBLE CRUST FOR A 20-23-CM/8-9-INCH PIE PLATE)

THE CLASSIC WAY

Sift the flour and salt together into a large mixing bowl and rub in the butter (1).

Mix the egg yolks with the water and add to the bowl (2), stirring to bind to a firm but malleable dough (3).

On a lightly floured surface, knead lightly until smooth, then shape into a flattened ball (4). Wrap in clingfilm/plastic wrap and chill for at least 30 minutes before rolling out and using in the recipe.

THE FOOD PROCESSOR METHOD

Sift the flour and salt together into the bowl of the machine.

Add the butter and process for about 30 seconds until the mixture resembles very fine breadcrumbs. Mix the egg yolks with 2 tablespoons of the water, pour into the food processor and pulse for 10 seconds. The dough should start to come together in large raggy lumps. If not, add another tablespoon of water and pulse again.

As soon as the dough forms one big lump (don't overprocess or the pastry will be tough), tip out onto a lightly floured surface and knead lightly. Shape into a flattened ball, wrap in clingfilm/plastic wrap and chill for at least 30 minutes before rolling out and using in the recipe.

ROUGH PUFF PASTRY

This is the quick way to make a good puff pastry. Needless to say, you must work very quickly, and it takes a little practice. Rolling and folding the pastry dough creates layers of pastry and pockets of butter. The cooked pastry will be buttery, puffy and light if made well, and *incomparable* to store-bought puff pastry. Make a large quantity at one time and freeze the remainder – it is easier to make in bulk and you will always have some on hand! A dash of lemon juice is sometimes added to strengthen the layers of dough.

250 g/2 cups plain/
all-purpose flour

a pinch of salt

150 g/10 tablespoons unsalted
butter, chilled

about 150 ml/⅔ cup ice-cold
water

**MAKES ABOUT 550 G/1¼ LBS.
(ENOUGH TO LINE OR MAKE A 30-CM/
12-INCH PIE PLATE OR BASE)**

Sift the flour and salt together into a large mixing bowl.

Quickly cut the butter into small cubes, about the size of the top of your little finger.

Stir the butter into the flour with a round-bladed knife so that it is evenly distributed (1).

Drizzle the water over the surface, then mix with the knife (2) until the dough starts to come together in a messy lump (3).

Tip out onto a lightly floured surface and knead lightly until it forms a streaky, rather lumpy ball. Flatten the ball with the palm of your hand (4) and wrap in clingfilm/plastic wrap. Chill for 30 minutes until firm. (Continued overleaf.)

ROUGH PUFF CONTINUED

Unwrap the chilled pastry and, on a lightly
floured surface, roll out away from you (5) into
a long rectangle, three times longer than it is wide
(no exact measurements needed here, but it
should be about 1 cm/½ inch thick). Mark the
pastry lightly into 3 equal sections with a blunt
knife. Now fold the third closest to you up over
the middle third (6). Brush off any excess flour
with a dry pastry brush (7), then bring the top
third over towards you to cover the folded two
thirds (8).

Give the pastry a quarter turn anti-clockwise
so that it looks like a closed book. Seal the edges
lightly with a rolling pin to stop them sliding out
of shape (9). Now roll out, always away from you
in one direction, until it is the same-sized rectangle
as before (10). Fold in the bottom (11) and top
(12) thirds in the same way as before, wrap in
clingfilm/plastic wrap and chill for 15 minutes.
Do this rolling and folding four more times, then
the pastry is ready to use in the recipe (13).

CHEAT'S ROUGH PUFF PASTRY

A great friend showed me how to do this and it is so easy – but the butter or margarine must be very hard. It is made in exactly the same way as the Rough Puff Pastry, except you freeze and grate the butter, then roll and fold the dough as quickly as you can. He swears that it is lighter made with margarine – I like butter!

250 g/2 cups plain/all-purpose flour

a pinch of salt

150 g/10 tablespoons unsalted butter, chilled

about 150 ml/⅔ cup ice-cold water

MAKES ABOUT 550 G/1¼ LBS. (ENOUGH TO LINE OR MAKE A 30-CM/12-INCH PIE PLATE OR BASE)

Sift the flour and salt together into a large mixing bowl.

Hold the butter in a dish towel or oven gloves, and quickly grate the butter into the flour. Stir in with a round-bladed knife so that it is evenly distributed.

Drizzle the water over the surface then mix with the knife until the dough starts to come together in a messy lump.

Tip out onto a lightly floured surface and knead lightly until it forms a streaky, rather lumpy ball. Flatten the ball with the palm of your hand and wrap in clingfilm/plastic wrap. Chill for 30 minutes until firm.

Only roll and fold a couple of times – no more, then wrap and chill for at least 30 minutes before rolling out and using in the recipe.

FRENCH BUTTER PIE PASTRY (PÂTE Á PÂTE)

Typically, this style of pastry is used for raised meat pies. Don't be tempted to leave out the water – adding it makes the pastry easier to handle in the end.

300 g/2⅓ cups plain/
all-purpose flour

½ teaspoon salt

200 g/13 tablespoons salted
butter, soft

2 egg yolks

3 tablespoons ice-cold water

**MAKES ABOUT 500 G/1 LB. 2 OZ.
(ENOUGH TO LINE AND DECORATE
A 1.5-LITRE/QUART PIE MOULD OR
A LOAF PAN MEASURING 23 CM/
9 INCHES LONG X 10 CM/4 INCHES
WIDE X 7.5 CM/3 INCHES DEEP)**

THE CLASSIC WAY

Sift the flour and salt into a mound on a clean surface (1). Make a well in the middle with your fist (2). Place the butter and egg yolks in the well (3) and, using the fingers of one hand, 'peck' the eggs and butter together until they resemble scrambled eggs (4). Flick the flour over the egg mixture (5) and chop it through with a palette knife until almost amalgamated. Sprinkle with the water (6) and chop again (7). Bring together quickly with your hands (8) and knead lightly into a smooth ball. Flatten (9), wrap in clingfilm/plastic wrap and chill for at least 30 minutes. Bring to room temperature before rolling out and using in the recipe.

IN THE FOOD PROCESSOR

This works well if you are scared of making pastry or have very hot hands, like me! Sift the flour and salt onto a sheet of baking parchment. Put the butter and egg yolks in the food processor (10) and blend until smooth. Add the water and blend again. Shoot in the flour (11) and work until just combined (12). Turn out onto a lightly floured surface and knead lightly until smooth. Form into a flattened ball, wrap in clingfilm/plastic wrap and chill for at least 30 minutes. Bring to room temperature before rolling out and using in the recipe.

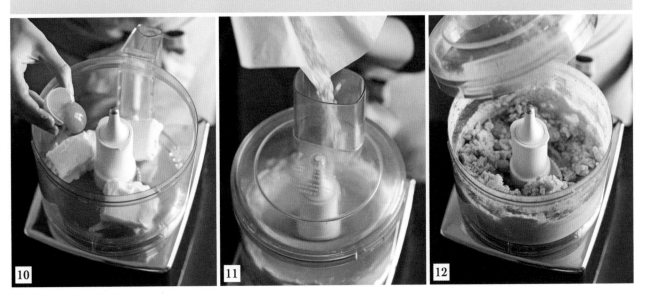

10 11 12

AMERICAN PIE CRUST

This is a recipe for the classic American Pie Crust given to me by a friend from NY State. She makes and bakes one to use, and freezes the other to be baked later. You could make and bake both and freeze to use later, or make a double quantity and freeze them all unbaked! To give the crust a richer flavour and golden colour, unsalted butter can be substituted for the cooking fat, or use half butter and half cooking fat (or pure lard).

Sift the flour and salt into a large mixing bowl and cut in the fat with two round-bladed knives (1) until thoroughly combined (2). (You can also do this in a food processor.)

In a separate bowl, mix together the beaten egg, vinegar and water. Pour this wet mixture into the dry mixture (3) and cut it in with the knives again (4).

Tip out onto a lightly floured surface and knead lightly until smooth (or knead it in the bowl), then shape into a flattened ball. Wrap in clingfilm/plastic wrap and chill for at least 30 minutes before rolling out and using in the recipe.

TIP: The uncooked dough can be frozen in flattened balls, ready to thaw and roll out as required.

375 g/3 cups plain/
all-purpose flour

a good pinch of salt

250 g/1 cup plus 2 tablespoons
white cooking fat/shortening,
chilled and diced

1 egg, beaten

1 tablespoon white wine vinegar

4 tablespoons ice-cold water

MAKES ABOUT 700 G/1 LB. 9 OZ.
(ENOUGH TO LINE THE BASE OF TWO
23-CM/9-INCH PIE PLATES OR MAKE
A 23-CM/9-INCH DOUBLE-CRUST PIE)

RICH HOT-WATER CRUST

I learned to make hot-water crust pastry at Leiths School of Food and Wine in the 1970s, and their recipe is still the best. Traditional Scottish hot-water crust is just flour, salt, lard and water – simple and delicious when chomping through a meat pie, but a bit insipid for richer recipes, so this is an enriched version. It is important to work quickly when making this; wrap and chill it, then bring it to room temperature before using. It will be much more malleable this way.

Sift the flour and salt together into a mixing bowl. Make a well in the centre and pour in the eggs (1), flicking a little flour over the top (2).

Put the lard (and butter), milk and water into a saucepan and slowly bring to the boil. Do not let it boil before the fat is melted. Pour the boiling liquid into the flour (3) and mix with a round-bladed knife (4).

Tip out onto a lightly floured surface and knead lightly until smooth and no longer streaky. Wrap in clingfilm/plastic wrap and chill for at least 30 minutes before rolling out and using in the recipe.

450 g/3⅔ cups plain/all-purpose flour

1 teaspoon salt

2 eggs, beaten

160 g/⅔ cup lard (or half lard, half butter)

100 ml/6 tablespoons water

100 ml/6 tablespoons milk

MAKES ABOUT 900 G/2 LBS.
(ENOUGH TO MAKE TWO DECORATED RAISED PIES OR 6–8 10-CM/4-INCH SMALL PIE CRUSTS)

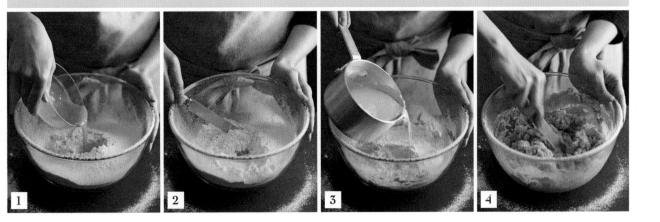

EVERYDAY PIES

STEAK AND KIDNEY PIE

My father loved to have lunch at Rules when he went to the city on business. As the oldest restaurant in London, founded in 1798, it knows its traditional British classics. His favourite dish of all was their glorious steak and kidney pie. Somehow he came back with the recipe and I used to make it every week when I worked in a shooting lodge. It is so easy to make, as the meat requires no browning, and I add really dark stock to give it colour. It is the best steak and kidney pie I have ever tasted. Add a dash of mushroom ketchup to it, or even Worcestershire sauce, for added flavour.

FOR THE PASTRY:

175 g/1½ sticks salted butter, chilled and cubed

350 g/2¾ cups self-raising flour

salt, to taste

200 ml/¾ cup cold whole milk, plus extra to glaze

FOR THE FILLING:

4 lamb's kidneys

750 g/1 lb. 10 oz. stewing beef, diced (preferably Galloway!)

250 g/9 oz. dark open-cup mushrooms

1 large onion, finely chopped

4–6 tablespoons chopped fresh parsley

1 tablespoon chopped fresh thyme

½ teaspoon crumbled bay leaves

1–2 tablespoons plain/all-purpose flour

600 ml/2½ cups dark beef stock

1 tablespoon English mustard powder

salt and freshly ground black pepper

a 1.5-litre/quart oval pie dish
a pie funnel

SERVES 6

Preheat the oven to 170°C (325°F) Gas 3.

For the filling, prepare the kidneys by splitting them in half and snipping out and discarding the creamy core. Slice or roughly chop the kidneys and add them to a large mixing bowl with the diced beef, mushrooms, onion, herbs, flour and plenty of salt and pepper.

In a separate bowl, combine the beef stock and mustard powder, stirring until the powder has dissolved, then pour into the mixing bowl with the other ingredients. Stir thoroughly and then pile the filling into the pie dish, pushing the pie funnel into the centre – it should fill the dish generously.

Now make the pastry. Put the butter, flour and salt into a large mixing bowl and use a round-bladed knife to chop and cut the butter into the flour until it resembles rough breadcrumbs. Stir in the milk and mix to a soft dough.

Tip the dough out onto a lightly floured surface and roll out to an oval shape that is slightly larger than the top of the dish. Cut off an extra long strip of pastry that will fit around the lip of the pie dish. Brush the lip of the pie dish with milk and press the pastry strip around the lip. Brush this with milk and lay the pastry oval over the dish, letting it fall on top of the pie funnel in the centre. Cut a cross in the pastry touching the pie funnel and gently push it over the funnel. Press the pastry onto the lip of the dish to seal and trim off the excess pastry. Crimp the pastry together and then brush the top of the pie with milk.

Stand the pie dish in a baking pan and bake in the preheated oven for 1¾ hours until golden and bubbling.

LAMB SHANK SHEPHERD'S PIE

Lamb shanks are one of those flavoursome, slow-cook cuts that I have found make a fantastic shepherd's pie – much more tasty than the usual minced/ground lamb. They are best cooked on the bone, the rich gelatinous connective tissue and marrow melting during the slow-cooking, adding richness to the sauce. To make it worthwhile, I cook a batch of 6–8 lamb shanks in a big slow cooker and freeze the meat once I've taken it off the bone and mixed it with the vegetables and sauce. This way, I always have a meal or two ready to whip out and finish off with mash at the end of the day.

2 tablespoons sunflower oil

4 large, meaty lamb shanks

1 onion, chopped

1 carrot, chopped

1 celery stick, chopped

1 generous tablespoon plain/all-purpose flour

1 litre/4 cups lamb or beef stock

1 tablespoon Worcestershire sauce

a few sprigs of fresh rosemary

a few sprigs of fresh thyme

FOR THE MASH TOPPING:

450 g/1 lb. carrots, roughly chopped

675 g/1½ lbs. potatoes, cut into chunks

50 g/3 tablespoons butter, plus extra to finish

about 100 ml/scant ½ cup hot milk

salt and freshly ground black pepper

a deep ovenproof dish

SERVES 4–6

Heat the oil in a deep flameproof casserole or heavy pan and brown the lamb shanks, 2 at a time, over a high heat – this will add to the colour and flavour. Lift out onto a plate with a slotted spoon, then add the onion, carrot and celery and cook for 5 minutes until the vegetables are beginning to brown. Add the flour and stir over a high heat for a couple of minutes until everything starts to brown and smell good.

Put the shanks back into the casserole and pour in the stock and Worcestershire sauce. Add the rosemary and thyme sprigs and season well with salt and pepper. Bring to the boil, then turn down the heat, cover and simmer for about 2 hours until the meat is falling off the bone. Alternatively, you can cook this in a slow cooker.

While the shanks are cooking, prepare the mash topping. Boil the carrots and the potatoes in plenty of salted water until tender (about 20 minutes), then drain. Mash the potatoes roughly with half the butter, the hot milk and salt and pepper. In a separate bowl, mash the carrots with the remaining butter. Cover both bowls and set aside until required.

Preheat the oven to 190°C (375°F) Gas 5.

When the lamb shanks are cooked, lift them out of the casserole and strip the meat off the bones. Skim the fat from the sauce left in the casserole, then stir the de-boned meat back in. Taste and season, then pile into the ovenproof dish.

Spread a layer of mashed carrot on top of the lamb in the dish and top that with a layer of potato, roughing up the surface. Dot with butter, set the pie on a baking sheet and bake in the preheated oven for 25–30 minutes until brown and bubbling.

FOR THE SUET CRUST PASTRY:

225 g/1¾ cups plain/all-purpose flour

½ teaspoon salt

50 g/2½ tablespoons lard

50 g/4 tablespoons shredded beef or vegetable suet

1 teaspoon dried mixed herbs

2–3 tablespoons ice-cold water

3–4 tablespoons milk, to glaze

FOR THE FILLING:

450 g/1 lb. cooked ham, diced

3 tablespoons plain/all-purpose flour, seasoned with salt and black pepper

2 tablespoons soft light brown sugar

¼ teaspoon freshly grated nutmeg

¼ teaspoon ground allspice

450 g/1 lb. cooking apples, peeled, cored and quartered

2 onions, thinly sliced

300 ml/1¼ cups dry (hard) cider

salt and freshly ground black pepper

a 900-ml/1-quart pie dish

a pie funnel

SERVES 4–6

HAM AND APPLE PIE

Serve this with a robust vegetable such as broccoli, cabbage or sprouts and boiled, buttered new potatoes. Cook in deep individual dishes if you have the time.

Preheat the oven to 200°C (400°F) Gas 6.

To make the pastry, sift the flour and salt into a large mixing bowl, add the lard and rub in with your fingertips until combined. Stir in the suet and herbs and mix to a soft dough with just enough of the water to bind. Knead lightly until smooth, then leave to rest in a cool place until required.

Toss the diced ham in the seasoned flour to lightly coat. Mix the sugar and spices together in a separate bowl.

Put half the ham in the pie dish and cover with half the apples, then half the spice mixture and half the onion slices. Repeat these layers, seasoning between each one, then pour in the cider.

On a lightly floured surface, roll out the pastry and make a small slit in the centre to fit over the pie funnel. Dampen the edges of the pie dish with a little milk and cover with the pastry. Brush the pastry with milk, set the pie dish on a baking sheet and bake in the preheated oven for 20 minutes. Reduce the temperature to 180°C (350°F) Gas 4 and bake for a further hour until golden (covering the top with kitchen foil if you feel the pastry is becoming too dark).

SIMPLE SAUSAGE LATTICE SLICE

This is an all-time family favourite that doesn't take long to make and that everyone loves. You can buy sausagemeat in most supermarkets or you can make your own with minced/ground pork and bacon. Or, if pushed for time, use your favourite butcher's sausages and squeeze them out of their skins. The lattice is easy to make once you get the hang of it. There are gadgets called lattice rollers, but I find these too fiddly and delicate for this. Spicy baked beans are the perfect accompaniment – don't try anything fancy with this; it's just not the same!

2 tablespoons lard or vegetable oil

1 small onion, finely chopped

400 g/14 oz. good sausagemeat (or your favourite sausages squeezed out of their skins)

1 teaspoon dried mixed herbs

2 tablespoons mango chutney

1 tablespoon Dijon mustard

1 teaspoon garlic salt (optional)

1 quantity Basic Shortcrust Pastry (see page 22), made with all lard

1 egg, beaten with a pinch of salt, to glaze

salt and freshly ground black pepper

SERVES 4

Preheat the oven to 200°C (400°F) Gas 6.

Melt the lard or heat the oil in a large saucepan set over medium heat, add the onion and fry until it is soft and translucent. Transfer to a large mixing bowl and add the sausagemeat, herbs, chutney, mustard, garlic salt (if using) and plenty of pepper. Using your hands or a wooden spoon, work it all together until evenly mixed.

On a lightly floured surface, roll out the pastry to a 32 x 32-cm/ 13 x 13-inch square and slide it onto a baking sheet.

Shape the sausagemeat into a log about 7.5 cm/3 inches wide and lay it in the centre of the pastry, leaving a 2-finger's-width margin at either end. Make 7–8 evenly-spaced diagonal cuts in the pastry along the 2 long sides of the sausagemeat filling.

Dampen the edges of the pastry with a little water. Fold each unslashed pastry edge over the ends of the sausagemeat, and then fold over the long sides, overlapping the cut pieces to give a plaited/ braided effect. Brush the slice with the beaten egg for a shiny glaze.

Bake in the preheated oven for about 40 minutes until the pastry is crisp and golden, and the sausagemeat is cooked right through. Slice and serve hot.

CHICKEN POT PIE

Ever since my mother received the legendary American cookery book *The Joy of Cooking* from my Canadian aunt to go with her brand new enormous Moffat cooker in the 1960s, we have had Chicken Pot Pie for Christmas Eve supper. It was always in front of the fire with the angel chimes lit for the first time. It was a magical start to the celebrations. Mum used a biscuit or scone topping (there are two versions of this pie!) and the filling was a velouté sauce enriched with cream and had whatever vegetables were in season or available. We sometimes had canned tuna in it instead of chicken. My version of it is designed to be quick comfort food, so if the crème fraîche doesn't appeal, replace with a white sauce or whatever you prefer.

55 g/4 tablespoons butter

1 large leek, trimmed and sliced

2 carrots, peeled and diced

450 g/1 lb. skinless, boneless chicken breast, cubed

about 8 leaves of fresh tarragon, chopped

3 tablespoons chopped fresh parsley

150 g/generous 1 cup fresh or frozen peas

250 ml/1 cup crème fraîche or double/heavy cream

1 quantity Rough Puff Pastry (see page 25) or Cheat's Puff Pastry (see page 27)

2 egg yolks, lightly beaten with a pinch of salt, to glaze

salt and freshly ground black pepper

4 x 250-ml/1-cup ovenproof dishes

SERVES 4

Melt the butter in a medium saucepan and add the leek and carrots. Cook for about 10 minutes or until they are both soft and cooked through. Add the chicken, stir well and cook for about 10 minutes until the chicken is cooked through. Stir in the tarragon and parsley, followed by the peas and crème fraîche. Bring to the boil, then remove from the heat and set aside.

Roll out the pastry on a lightly floured surface and cut four round discs at least 2.5 cm/1 inch wider than the diameter of your ovenproof dishes.

Spoon the chicken filling evenly into the dishes, brush the edges of the dishes with a little beaten egg yolk and top each with a pastry round. Press the pastry firmly down onto the edges of the dishes to seal. You may like to crimp or fork the edges, but keep it fairly casual. (There's need for a hole in the lid of these – the puff pastry wants to rise up into a dome.) Brush with beaten egg yolk and chill for at least 30 minutes.

Preheat the oven to 200°C (400°F) Gas 6.

Remove the pies from the fridge, brush with more beaten egg yolk (thinned down with a little water or milk if necessary) to build up a nice glaze, then set them on a large baking sheet. Bake in the preheated oven for about 20 minutes or until the pastry tops are puffed and golden brown and the pies are bubbling hot inside.

CHICKEN AND MUSHROOM PIE

Simple to make and one of the very best everyday pies, this dish is made all the more delicious by the addition of mushroom ketchup, a deeply-flavoured seasoning sauce. It is not thick or tomato-based like classic ketchup and is used to enrich meat, poultry and game dishes. Alternatively you can use Worcestershire or even soy sauce – all these sauces will add a deep savouriness to the dish.

4 skinless, boneless chicken thighs

2 large skinless, boneless chicken breasts

100 g/3½ oz. bacon lardons (or 3 slices of lean slab bacon, sliced into short strips)

1 onion, thinly sliced

100 g/3½ oz. chestnut/cremini mushrooms, quartered or thickly sliced

3 tablespoons chopped fresh parsley

2 teaspoons mushroom ketchup, Worcestershire sauce or soy sauce

4 tablespoons chicken stock

½ quantity Basic Shortcrust Pastry (see page 22)

1 egg, beaten with a pinch of salt, to glaze

salt and freshly ground black pepper

a 900-ml/1-quart, deep pie dish

a pie fiunnel

SERVES 4-6

Preheat the oven to 190°C (375°F) Gas 5 and place the pie funnel in the centre of the dish.

Cut the chicken into large pieces and mix with the bacon lardons/strips. Layer the chicken mixture into the pie dish with the onion, mushrooms, parsley, salt and pepper. Mix the mushroom ketchup (or alternative) with the chicken stock and pour over the filling.

Roll out the pastry on a lightly floured surface, making sure it is not too thin. Make a small hole in the centre of the pastry to fit over the pie funnel and use it to cover the pie. Crimp, scallop or fork the edges to seal. Brush with beaten egg and bake in the preheated oven for 1½ hours until golden.

RICOTTA AND GREEN HERB TORTA

Torta usually means 'cake' in Italy, but in the Lunigiana and Liguria regions a torta is a filled savoury pie containing greens (or vegetables) and cheese, which can be served either as an appetizer or as a main course. They are normally eaten at room temperature in order to appreciate the delicate flavours. Balance the more assertive-flavoured greens with milder ones. Try using a mix of beetroot tops/beet greens, spinach or Swiss chard or even spring greens mixed with peppery rocket/arugula, mustard greens and some watercress. Sometimes I make this torta in a free-form way, straight onto a baking sheet, for a truly homemade look. It is delicious served with a tomato and red onion salad and a pile of fresh salad leaves.

FOR THE ITALIAN OLIVE OIL PASTRY:

500 g/4 cups plain/all-purpose flour (Italian 00 if possible)

1–2 teaspoons fine sea salt

4 tablespoons extra virgin olive oil, plus extra to drizzle

150 ml/⅔ cup warm water

FOR THE FILLING:

500 g/1 lb. mixed greens

30 g/2 tablespoons unsalted butter

½ onion, very finely chopped

200 g/7 oz. ricotta, soft goats' cheese or cream cheese

140 g/2 cups grated Parmesan

2 teaspoons plain/all-purpose flour

2 tablespoons chopped fresh marjoram

3 large eggs, beaten

salt and freshly ground black pepper

a 30-cm/12-inch loose-based baking pan, 2.5 cm/1 inch deep, lightly oiled

SERVES 6-8

To make the pastry, put the flour in a large mixing bowl and make a well in the middle with your fist. Add the salt and the olive oil, then pour in 150 ml/⅔ cup warm water, a little at a time (you may not need it all). Mix to form a soft dough, then use your hands to bring it together, kneading it gently into a ball for about 2 minutes – just long enough to become smooth to the touch (this is totally different to normal pastry!). Seal the dough in a plastic bag and leave to rest for 1 hour at room temperature.

Preheat the oven to 190°C (375°F) Gas 5.

Wash the greens and remove any tough stems. While still wet, steam the greens using only the water that clings to their leaves. Squeeze them dry and chop coarsely.

Melt the butter in a small saucepan set over medium heat, add the onion and cook until soft and translucent. Stir in the chopped greens and cook for 2–3 minutes to heat through and coat with the butter. Remove the pan from the heat, leave to cool, then transfer the onion and greens to a large mixing bowl and beat in the ricotta, Parmesan, flour, marjoram, eggs, salt and plenty of pepper.

Once the pastry dough has rested, cut it into 2 pieces (one slightly larger than the other) and roll each piece out as thinly as you can on a lightly floured surface. Use the larger piece to line the pan, making sure that the pastry overhangs the edges.

Fill the lined pan with the cheese and greens mix, then cover with the remaining sheet of pastry. Press the edges together and trim off the excess dough. Crimp or turn the edges inwards in a rope fashion to seal the pie – it should look quite rustic! Make a couple of long slits in the top with a sharp knife. Drizzle a little olive oil on top of the crust and bake in the preheated oven for 40 minutes or until the crust is set and golden.

Serve warm or at room temperature.

PASTA, PARMESAN AND CHERRY TOMATO PIES

This is my take on the classic Scottish macaroni pie or 'peh'. I always wanted to like them, but never found a good one, so I make my own now! These are delicious served freshly baked out of the oven. Commercially, the pie shells are stamped out in a metal die and left to dry out for 24–48 hours to make them robust enough to bake and not collapse. This type of pie always has a 1-cm/½-inch rim of pastry extending above the filling to provide a space for adding extra mashed potatoes, baked beans, brown sauce or gravy. These are delicious served freshly baked out of the oven.

1 quantity Rich Hot-water Crust (see page 31)

110 g/4 oz. (about 1 cup) dried pasta shapes (such as smaller rigatoni, fusilli, tubetti or macaroni)

40 g/3 tablespoons butter

2½ tablespoons plain/all-purpose flour

a pinch of cayenne pepper

a pinch of English mustard powder

350 ml/1½ cups milk

100 g/1½ cups grated strong Cheddar cheese

30 cherry or baby plum tomatoes, halved

50 g/⅔ cup grated Parmesan

salt and freshly ground black pepper

6 x 10-cm/4-inch straight-sided ramekins, jars, chef's rings or other small pie moulds

MAKES 6

Start making the pie crusts the day before. Follow the recipe on page 31, and while the pastry is chilling, cover the chosen pie moulds with clingfilm/plastic wrap.

Divide the pastry dough into 6 pieces. On a lightly floured surface, roll out each piece thinly, drape over the upturned base of each mould and smooth gently to fit. Don't worry about uneven edges – these will be trimmed off later. Set on a tray and chill or freeze for 30 minutes. When firmly set, use a sharp knife to trim the pastry on each one to 5 cm/2 inches deep. Carefully ease the pie crusts out of the moulds and pull out the clingfilm/plastic wrap. Set the pie crusts on a tray and leave to dry out in a cool dry place for 24 hours.

Preheat the oven to 200°C (400°F) Gas 6.

Cook the pasta according to the package instructions. While the pasta is cooking, melt the butter in a medium saucepan and add the flour, cayenne pepper and mustard. Cook, stirring, for 1 minute. Remove from the heat. Pour in the milk and whisk in well. Return to the heat and stir until boiling. Simmer, stirring all the time, for 2 minutes.

Drain the pasta well and stir into the sauce. Season to taste and stir in the grated Cheddar. Set aside and leave to cool until tepid.

Spoon the pasta sauce into the dried pie crusts, leaving enough of a rim of pastry projecting above to hold the tomatoes. Pile the tomato halves over the surface of the pies and sprinkle with the Parmesan. Stand the pies in a shallow baking pan and bake in the preheated oven for 10–15 minutes to set the pastry. Reduce the oven temperature to 180°C (350°F) Gas 4 and bake for a further 20 minutes, or until golden and bubbling.

CREAMY MUSHROOM PLATE PIE

I am lucky enough to live in the Scottish countryside and have my secret places where wild mushrooms, particularly chanterelles/girolles, grow in abundance. However, I have also found smoky black trompettes de mort, many types of ceps (boletus), hedgehog mushrooms and violet deceivers. With this abundance, there is nothing for it but to dry most of them to preserve them for later and make a pie. This pie can be made with cultivated mushrooms, fresh wild mushrooms or a mix of dried and fresh – whatever you can lay your hands on! However, do try to use mace in the sauce – it is really special. Serve with a peppery green salad.

300 ml/1¼ cups whole milk

1 blade of mace (or a grating of fresh nutmeg)

3 sprigs of fresh thyme

1 bay leaf

6 peppercorns

1 quantity Rich Shortcrust Pastry (see page 24)

50 g/3 tablespoons butter

1 large onion or 4 large banana shallots, thinly sliced

225 g/8 oz. mixed fresh mushrooms (such as dark open-cup, chestnut/cremini or shiitake), sliced

3 tablespoons plain/all-purpose flour

3 tablespoons double/heavy cream (optional)

1 egg yolk

25 g/½ cup grated Parmesan

1 small egg, beaten with a pinch of salt, to glaze

salt and freshly ground black pepper

a 23-cm/9-inch round enamel pie plate

mushroom and leaf pasty cutters

SERVES 4-6

Put the milk, mace, thyme, bay leaf and peppercorns in a medium saucepan and bring to the boil. (If you are using dried mushrooms, you can add them to the milk with the flavourings so that they will soften.) Remove from the heat and leave to infuse while you line the pie plate.

Roll out the pastry thinly on a lightly floured surface. Use the rolling pin to pick up the pastry and drape it over the pie plate. Ease the pastry into the plate and trim the edge with a sharp knife, reserving the trimmings for decoration. Chill the pie and trimmings.

Preheat the oven to 200°C (400°F) Gas 6 and set a heavy baking sheet on the middle shelf to heat.

Melt the butter in a large saucepan and add the sliced onion and 2 tablespoons of water. Cook slowly for about 10 minutes until soft but without browning, then add the mushrooms and increase the heat. Cook briskly for 2–3 minutes, stirring occasionally until the mushrooms are wilted. Remove from the heat, stir in the flour and set aside for a moment.

Strain the infused milk into a jug/pitcher. (If you have added dried mushrooms to the milk, carefully pick the mace, thyme, bay leaf and peppercorns from the sieve/strainer and tip the soaked dried mushrooms into the pan with the fresh ones.) Gradually stir the milk into the mushrooms, blending thoroughly. Return the pan to the heat and stir until boiling. Remove from the heat again, add the cream and egg yolk and season well with salt and pepper. Turn the mushroom mix out onto a metal tray to cool.

Once the filling is cold, remove the pie plate from the fridge and lightly prick the base all over. Spoon in the filling, spreading evenly.

Roll out the pastry trimmings and stamp out shapes with the cutters to decorate the top and/or edges of the pastry. Brush the pastry with the beaten egg, then sprinkle the pie with the Parmesan. Set the pie on the baking sheet in the preheated oven and bake for 25–35 minutes until golden. Serve warm or cold from the plate.

RICOTTA, SAUSAGE AND POTATO PIZZA PIE

I make this whilst the antique wood-fired oven is firing up during our pizza lesson up at the old farmhouse in Sicily and we all tuck in as soon as it appears from the fiery mouth of the oven. However, it works well baked in a nice hot domestic oven.

FOR THE SICILIAN PIZZA DOUGH:

7 g/¼ oz. fresh yeast, 1 teaspoon dried active baking yeast, or ½ teaspoon fast-action yeast

a pinch of sugar

150 ml/⅔ cup hand-hot water

250 g/2 cups fine semolina flour (*farina di semola*) or durum wheat flour

½ teaspoon fine sea salt

1 tablespoon olive oil, plus extra for brushing

1 tablespoon freshly squeezed lemon juice

FOR THE FILLING:

2 tablespoons extra virgin olive oil

200 g/7 oz. potatoes, finely diced

2 onions, finely chopped

2 teaspoons dried oregano

250 g/9 oz. fresh Italian sausages, skinned

2 teaspoons tomato purée/paste

1 teaspoon fennel seeds

2 tablespoons chopped fresh sage

3 large eggs, beaten

125 g/4½ oz. ricotta

salt and freshly ground black pepper

a large lipless baking sheet

SERVES 6–8

In a medium bowl, cream the yeast with the sugar and whisk in the water. Leave for 10 minutes until frothy. (For other yeasts, use according to manufacturer's instructions.)

Sift the flour and salt into a mixing bowl and make a well in the centre. Pour in the yeast mixture, oil and lemon juice. Mix with a round-bladed knife, then your hands until the dough comes together. Add more water if necessary – the dough should be very soft.

Tip out onto a lightly floured surface and knead briskly for at least 10 minutes until smooth, shiny and elastic. Try not to add any extra flour at this stage – a wetter dough is better. If you feel that the dough is sticky, flour your hands and not the dough. It should be quite soft, but if *really* too soft to handle, knead in a little more flour. When ready, shape into a neat ball, place in a clean, oiled bowl, cover with a damp dish towel and leave to rise in a warm place until doubled in size – about 1½ hours.

Punch the air out of the dough, then transfer to a floured surface. Divide into two pieces (one piece slightly larger than the other) and shape both into a smooth ball. Place the balls well apart on a sheet of floured non-stick baking parchment, cover with clingfilm/plastic wrap and leave to rise for 60–90 minutes.

Place the baking sheet on the lower shelf of the oven and preheat it to 220°C (425°F) Gas 7 for at least 30 minutes.

Heat the oil in a frying pan and add the potato and onion. Cook for 5–10 minutes until the onions start to colour, and the potato is soft (add a spoonful of water if the vegetables look as if they are drying out). Stir in the oregano, season and transfer to a bowl to cool. Fry the sausage very briefly, breaking it up with the back of a fork, and add the tomato purée/paste, fennel seeds and sage. Season well, then let cool. In a separate bowl, beat the eggs into the ricotta.

Punch the air out of the the dough again. Roll out the smaller ball (the base) to a 25-cm/10-inch circle and the larger piece (the lid) to a 30-cm/12-inch circle, rolling the dough directly onto baking parchment. Spoon the potato and onion mixture onto the base and dot with the sausage. Spoon over the ricotta and egg mix and season well. Brush the edge with water and lay the lid on top, rolling the edges to seal. Brush with a little olive oil and make two or three holes in the top of the pie.

Working quickly, open the oven door and slide parchment and all onto the hot baking sheet. Bake for 10 minutes, then pull the parchment out from beneath the pie. Bake for a further 25–30 minutes until the crust is puffed up and golden. Remove from the oven and brush with a little olive oil. Leave to stand for 5 minutes before serving.

GLORIOUS GOLDEN FISH PIE

This is a real British family favourite and is worth spending the time to get it just right. The secret of a well-flavoured moist and juicy fish pie is not to overcook the fish and not to pre-cook the prawns/shrimp. I like to cook the prawn/shrimp shells in a little milk flavoured with onion, bay leaves and parsley stalks to really extract all the sweet flavour from them. Use the driest, flouriest potatoes you can for the mash – if you cook them whole in the microwave or bake them in the oven, the scooped-out flesh will be nice and dry and perfect for mashing. You can make the mash without the saffron, but try it for a treat – it looks and tastes wonderful.

350 g/12 oz. raw shell-on tiger prawns/shrimp

700 ml/3 cups milk

1 onion, chopped

1 bay leaf

2 peppercorns

450 g/1 lb. fresh sustainable white fish fillets (such as cod, haddock pollack), skin on

450 g/1 lb. undyed smoked haddock or cod fillet, skin on

75 g/5 tablespoons butter

75 g/½ cup plus 1 tablespoon plain/all-purpose flour

4 tablespoons chopped fresh parsley

salt and freshly ground black pepper

FOR THE SAFFRON AND DILL MASH:

1.3 kg/3 lbs. floury potatoes, peeled

a large pinch of saffron threads soaked in 3 tablespoons hot water

75 g/5 tablespoons butter

250 ml/1 cup milk

3 tablespoons chopped fresh dill

a 1.5-litre/quart oval pie dish

SERVES 4–6

Peel the shells from the prawns/shrimp. Put the shells in a saucepan with the milk, onion, bay leaf and peppercorns. Bring to the boil then lower the heat and simmer for 10 minutes. Turn off the heat and set aside to infuse.

Lay the white and smoked fish fillets, skin side up, in a roasting pan. Strain the infused milk into the pan and and simmer on the hob/stovetop for 5–7 minutes until just opaque. Lift the fish fillets out of the milk and transfer to a plate. When the fillets are cool enough to handle, pull off the skin and flake the fish into large pieces, removing any bones as you go. Transfer to a large bowl and add the shelled prawns/shrimp.

Melt the butter in a small saucepan set over medium heat, stir in the flour and gradually add the flavoured milk from the roasting pan. Whisk well and simmer gently for 15 minutes until thick and a little reduced. Taste and season with salt and pepper. Stir in the parsley and pour the sauce over the fish. Carefully mix everything together, then transfer the mixture to the pie dish and leave to cool.

Preheat the oven to 180°C (350°F) Gas 4.

Boil the potatoes in salted water until soft, drain well and mash. Beat in the saffron and its soaking water (if using), butter, milk and dill. When the fish mixture is cold, spoon over the golden mash, piling it up gloriously on top. Bake in the preheated oven for 30–40 minutes or until the potato is golden brown and crispy. If it fails to brown enough, finish it off under a medium grill/broiler. Serve immediately!

SAVOURY VEGAN NUTTY PIE

300 g/10 oz. mixed nuts (such as brazil nuts, cashews, pecans)

75 g/½ cup pine nuts

75 g/½ cup pumpkin seeds

1 tablespoon black onion seeds (kalonji) (optional)

3 slices (about 200 g/7 oz.) sunflower seed rye bread

1 small onion, finely chopped

2 garlic cloves, crushed

3 tablespoons olive or rapeseed oil

1 tablespoon freeze-dried oregano (or 2 tablespoons fresh)

1 teaspoon dried thyme (or 2 teaspoons fresh)

1 teaspoon smoked paprika (pimenton)

1 carrot

1 sweet potato

2 celery sticks

2 tablespoons soy sauce

2 tablespoons sweet chilli sauce

425-g/14-oz. can chickpeas (or lentils) in water, drained

150 g/5½ oz. silken tofu, beaten

1 quantity Basic Shortcrust Pastry (vegan variation – see page 22)

100 g/¾ cup unsalted cashew nuts, toasted in the oven

50 g/scant ½ cup pine nuts, toasted in the oven

salt and freshly ground black pepper

FOR THE HONEY AND SOY GLAZE:

2 tablespoons Japanese soy sauce

1 tablespoon runny honey

a 23-cm/9-inch enamel pie plate

a baking sheet lined with non-stick baking parchment

SERVES 6–8

Making a really tasty vegan pie filling is not so difficult! If you balance flavours and textures of nuts, grains, pulses, vegetables and herbs, you can come up with something that no meat-eater would ever have to fear! Ring the changes by using hazelnuts or walnuts instead of pecans and vary the seeds by using a mixture of sunflower seeds, sesame seeds and flax seeds.

Pulse the mixed nuts in batches in a food processor until they are roughly ground, then tip into a large mixing bowl. Stir in the pine nuts, pumpkin seeds and black onion seeds (if using). Blitz the rye bread in the food processor until it forms breadcrumbs and add that to the nuts. Without rinsing the food processor bowl, blend the onion and garlic until finely chopped.

Heat the oil in a large deep frying pan and stir in the onion and garlic, along with the oregano, thyme and smoked paprika, then cook for 5 minutes while you grate the carrot, sweet potato and celery in the food processor. Add these to the frying pan, stir well to mix and cook for 10 minutes until soft but not coloured.

Remove from the heat and stir in the soy sauce and sweet chilli sauce, then the drained chickpeas. Tip all of this onto the nut mix and work together using a wooden spoon or your clean hands. Taste and season really well with salt and pepper. Finally, thoroughly mix in the beaten tofu and leave to cool.

On a lightly floured surface, roll out half the pastry dough and use it to line the pie plate. Roll out the second half of the dough to a rectangle and cut it into random triangles. Put the triangles onto the prepared baking sheet and chill until needed.

Preheat the oven to 220°C (425°F) Gas 7.

Spoon the cooled mix into the pie crust, smooth the top and lightly press down. Scatter the toasted cashews and pine nuts evenly over the surface. Now arrange the triangles randomly over the surface of the pie and its edges, overlapping and leaving gaps here and there. Chill for 20 minutes before baking in the preheated oven for about 40 minutes until firm and beginning to brown.

Mix the soy sauce with the honey in a saucapan and boil for 30 seconds to make a rich glaze. Brush the glaze over the pastry 5 minutes before the end of cooking and return the pie to the oven, watching carefully that it doesn't catch and burn. Remove from the oven and serve warm out of the pan.

TIP: You can make the filling the day before, then fill the pie and bake it on the day you want to eat it. The raw nut mix can also be used to make vegetarian or vegan sausage rolls or a nut Wellington. And it's even delicious eaten cold, like a rough pâté.

POSH PIES

MY 'AULD ALLIANCE' NEW YEAR STEAK PIE

In Scotland, piles of Steak or Ashet pies appear in butcher's windows ready for New Year's Day. Many French words appear in the Scots language and ashet (assiette) is one of them. The dish is a deep, rectangular, white enamel one, with a lip to support the pastry top (butcher's pies are made in thick crimped foil pans of a similar shape).

60 g/4 tablespoons unsalted butter or beef dripping

3 onions or 6 large shallots, sliced

25 g/1 oz. dried wild mushrooms (such as ceps or porcini), soaked in a little warm water for 20 minutes

900 g/2 lbs. boneless beef shoulder steak, trimmed and cut into 2.5-cm/1-inch cubes

40 g/⅓ cup plain/all-purpose flour

2 tablespoons olive oil

150 g/5½ oz. bacon lardons/finely diced country ham or Italian cubetti di pancetta

300 ml/1¼ cups good dark beef or game stock

300 ml/1¼ cups Scottish ale (not too dark)

2 bay leaves

1 tablespoon dried mixed Herbes de Provence (for the Auld Alliance!)

2–3 tablespoons chopped fresh parsley

1 quantity Rough Puff Pastry (see page 25) or Cheat's Puff Pastry (see page 27)

1 egg, beaten, to glaze

salt and freshly ground black pepper

a 1.5-litre/quart rectangular pie dish

a pie funnel

SERVES 6

Preheat the oven to 180°C (350°F) Gas 4.

Melt two-thirds of the butter or dripping in a large flameproof casserole until no longer sizzling. Add the onions or shallots and fry over a high heat for about 5 minutes until nicely golden, then remove the casserole from the heat.

Drain the wild mushrooms, adding the soaking water to the beef stock. Rinse and chop the mushrooms, then add them to the onions.

Put the beef into a plastic bag with the flour and some salt and pepper and toss together until the cubes are well coated.

Heat a large frying pan until hot. Add the olive oil, then stir-fry the bacon lardons/ham cubes for a few minutes until rich and golden. Remove with a slotted spoon and add to the onions in the casserole.

Melt the remaining butter or dripping in the frying pan, then quickly brown the beef well on all sides. Transfer to the casserole.

Now pour the stock and ale into the frying pan, bring to the boil and scrape up all the browned bits sticking to the bottom of the pan – these will help to flavour the gravy. Boil for 1–2 minutes, then pour into the casserole. Add the bay leaves, dried herbs and plenty of seasoning (especially pepper) and mix well.

Cover the casserole with a tight-fitting lid and bake in the preheated oven for 1–1½ hours until the meat is tender. Leave to cool completely, then chill.

To finish the pie, preheat the oven to 200°C (400°F) Gas 6.

Stir the chopped parsley into the chilled filling and spoon into the pie dish. Place a pie funnel in the centre of the dish.

Roll out the pastry on a lightly floured surface to a good 5 cm/2 inches bigger than the top of the dish. Line the rim of the dish with a thin strip of pastry and brush the pastry rim with the beaten egg. Lift the pastry lid over the dish, letting it fall on top of the pie funnel in the centre. Cut a cross in the pastry touching the pie funnel and gently push it over the funnel. Press the pastry onto the lip of the dish to seal and trim off the excess pastry with a small sharp knife. Knock up (see page 16), then crimp the edges to seal firmly. Use any pastry trimmings to decorate the top of the pie. Brush with more beaten egg and chill for 30 minutes or more. (This can all be done the day before.)

Just before cooking, brush the pastry once more with beaten egg. Set the pie on a baking sheet and bake in the preheated oven for 30–35 minutes until the pastry is risen and golden brown.

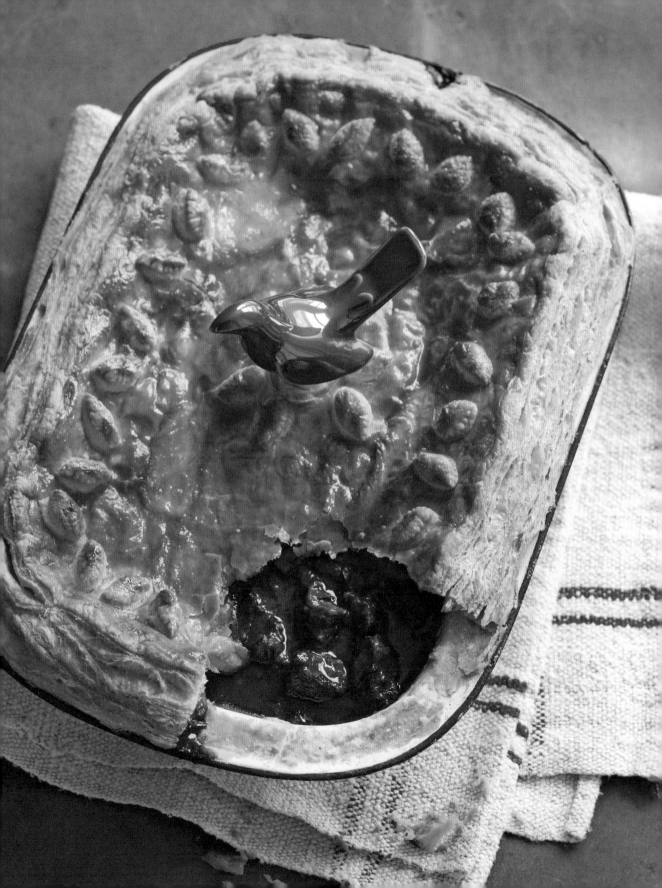

FILLET OF BEEF EN CROÛTE

This is also known as Beef Wellington and brings greedy smiles to all assembled faces around a dinner table. This is real special occasion stuff. Take a little time to decorate the surface of the pastry lavishly with pastry leaves, flowers, tassels, a birthday name, mushrooms – whatever takes your fancy. Just remember to give it two coats of salted egg wash with a drying period in between for a rich glossy sheen. The whole thing can be prepared well in advance (un-eggwashed), wrapped in kitchen foil and refrigerated until half an hour or so before cooking. Remove the foil and brush with egg before baking. This doesn't really freeze well.

1 quantity Rough Puff Pastry
(see page 25)

1 tablespoon olive oil

1.35-kg/3-lb. piece of beef fillet,
trimmed of fat and membrane

1 egg plus 1 yolk, beaten,
to glaze

FOR THE STUFFING:

55 g/4 tablespoons unsalted
butter

2 onions or 6 large banana
shallots, finely chopped

225 g/8 oz. dark open-cup
mushrooms, very finely chopped

2 teaspoons chopped fresh thyme

1 teaspoon finely grated
orange zest

1 tablespoon balsamic vinegar

100 g/3½ oz. chicken or duck
liver pâté

salt and freshly ground
black pepper

SERVES 6-8

Preheat the oven to 200°C (400°F) Gas 6.

To make the stuffing, melt the butter in a saucepan, add the onions and fry gently for 10 minutes until softening. Stir in the mushrooms and cook, stirring occasionally, for 10 minutes until soft and well-reduced (there should be no liquid left in the pan). Stir in the thyme, orange zest and vinegar, then cook for a further 1–2 minutes. Remove from the heat and beat in the pâté. Season well with salt and pepper and leave to cool completely (this can be made the night before and chilled).

On a lightly floured surface, roll out a third of the pastry to a strip about the size of the piece of fillet. Lift onto a heavy baking sheet, prick all over with a fork and bake in the preheated oven for about 20 minutes until golden brown and crisp. Remove from the oven to a wire rack and leave to cool.

Heat the oil in a frying pan or roasting pan until hot. Add the fillet and quickly brown all over, turning it often. Remove to a cold baking sheet and leave to cool.

When everything is cold, lay the cooked pastry strip on a baking sheet and place the fillet on top. Spoon the mushroom mixture over the top of the beef (or mould it thinly over the top and sides).

Preheat the oven to 230°C (450°F) Gas 8.

Roll out the remaining pastry to a piece large enough to cover the beef comfortably. Lay the pastry over the beef and neatly wrap it around the fillet, tucking the ends underneath with a fish slice, spatula or palette knife and trimming off any excess. Use the pastry trimmings to make shapes with which to decorate the top.

Brush with the beaten egg, decorate lavishly with the pastry shapes and bake in the preheated oven for 20 minutes. Cover the pastry loosely with kitchen foil to prevent further browning and continue to bake for a further 15 minutes. If the fillet is a thick one, this will cook it to medium rare. If the fillet is from the thin end, give it 25 minutes in total. Allow to rest in a warm place for 10–15 minutes before slicing to serve.

BEEF AND SMOKED OYSTER PIE

A favourite in Victorian times when oysters were plentiful and cheap (the original surf 'n' turf!). Nowadays, due to the prohibitive cost of fresh oysters, I add canned smoked oysters instead, which give a rich smokiness to the gravy. Serve with truffled mash and a fresh oyster on the side to slip under the crust to warm through.

900 g/2 lbs. beef shin, trimmed and cut into large chunks

2 tablespoons plain/all-purpose flour

3 tablespoons sunflower oil

1 onion, finely chopped

1 garlic clove, crushed

1 teaspoon tomato purée/paste

200 ml/¾ cup dark ale or stout

1.5 litres/6 cups dark rich beef stock

1 teaspoon chopped fresh lemon thyme

1 fresh bay leaf, plus 4–6 to decorate

1 tablespoon cornflour/cornstarch dissolved in a little milk (optional)

2 x 85-g/3-oz. cans smoked oysters in oil, drained well

salt and freshly ground black pepper

FOR THE LEMON AND PARSLEY CRUST:

225 g/1¾ cups self-raising flour

85 g/3 oz. shredded beef suet

55 g/4 tablespoons butter, chilled and grated or finely diced

1 teaspoon grated lemon zest

1 generous tablespoon chopped fresh parsley

freshly squeezed juice of ½ lemon

1 egg, beaten, to glaze

4–6 individual deep pie dishes

SERVES 4–6

Put the beef into a plastic bag with the flour and some salt and pepper and toss together until the cubes are well coated. Heat the oil in a large heavy frying pan or flameproof casserole and brown the meat in 2 or 3 batches over high heat. Remove from the pan and set aside.

Add the onion and garlic to the pan and fry for a few minutes until lightly coloured, then add the tomato purée/paste and ale. Stir until the tomato dissolves, then add the beef stock, thyme, bay leaf and browned beef. Bring up to the boil, cover with a lid and simmer gently for about 2 hours or until the meat is tender. Check the gravy and if not thick enough add a little of the cornflour/cornstarch mix and simmer for a further couple of minutes until thickened. Leave to cool completely before mixing in the smoked oysters. Fill the pie dishes with the filling to about 1 cm/½ inch from the top.

To make the pastry, sift the flour into a large mixing bowl and add the suet, butter, lemon zest and parsley. Put the lemon juice in a measuring jug/cup and top up with cold water to make 170 ml/⅔ cup liquid. Add the lemony water to the mixing bowl and quickly mix to a dough with a round-bladed knife. Tip onto a lightly floured surface and knead quickly until smooth.

Roll out the pastry on a lightly floured surface to about ¾ cm/¼ inch thick and cut out 4–6 pieces large enough to cover the pie dishes. Brush the edges of the pastry with a little of the beaten egg and lay the pastry on top of each filled dish, pressing the egged edges against the rim of the dishes to seal. Cut a 2-cm/¾-inch hole in the centre of each pie lid, brush well with beaten egg and stick a bay leaf at a jaunty angle into each hole. Leave to rest in a cool place for 30 minutes.

Preheat the oven to 200°C (400°F) Gas Mark 6.

Set the pies on a large baking sheet and bake in the preheated oven for 30–35 minutes or until the pastry is deeply golden.

500 g/4 cups plain/all-purpose flour

190 g/12½ tablespoons butter

170 g/¾ cup plus 2 tablespoons caster/granulated sugar

2 egg yolks mixed with 2 tablespoons cold water, to bind

FOR THE FILLING:

a 1.5-kg/3¼-lb. chicken, poached

1 egg, beaten

100 g/1½ cups grated Parmesan

3 tablespoons chopped fresh oregano

2 tablespoons olive oil

600 ml/2½ cups rich meat stock

2 tablespoons plain/all-purpose flour, plus extra for coating

½ teaspoon ground allspice or cinnamon

125 g/4 oz. fresh chicken livers, cleaned and chopped

125 g/4 oz. Parma ham/prosciutto crudo, cut into thin strips

25 g/1 oz. dried porcini mushrooms, soaked in warm water for 20 minutes

500 g/1 lb. dried penne, or similar

125 g/1 stick butter

10 quail's eggs, soft-boiled and peeled (see page 86)

2 egg yolks, beaten with a large pinch of salt, to glaze

1 sachet/envelope powdered saffron (optional)

salt and freshly ground black pepper

a 23-cm/9-inch springform cake pan, greased with butter

SERVES 8

ITALIAN MEDIEVAL EXTRAVAGANZA PIE

This is based on a traditional Sicilian recipe for a supreme 'timballo'. It ranks among the most sumptuous creations of the haute cuisine of a Sicilian French-trained 'monzu' chef. Serve with spinach sautéed with raisins and pine nuts.

Make the pastry following the method for Rich Shortcrust Pastry (see page 24), adding the sugar to the flour and salt. Divide the pastry into 2 pieces, approximately one-third and two-thirds, and chill for 30 minutes.

Strip the flesh from the cooked chicken, discarding the skin and bones. Tear the light meat into strips and reserve. Finely chop the dark meat and mix with the beaten egg, 75 g/1¼ cups of the Parmesan and the oregano. Season well, then shape into small meatballs. Toss these lightly in flour and fry them in the olive oil until nicely browned. Drain on paper towels and set aside.

In a small bowl, mix 3 tablespoons of the stock with the flour and spice until smooth. Pour the remaining stock into a saucepan and whisk in the stock and flour mixture. Slowly bring to the boil, then simmer gently for 5 minutes until slightly thickened and glossy. Stir in the reserved chicken strips, chicken livers, Parma ham and drained and chopped soaked porcini mushrooms and heat through for a few minutes. Season well.

Cook the pasta in plenty of salted boiling water until *very* al dente. Drain and toss with the butter, then add to the chicken mixture. Finally, stir in the remaining Parmesan and leave to cool.

Preheat the oven to 200°C (400°F) Gas 6.

On a lightly floured surface, roll out the larger piece of pastry and use to line the cake pan, pressing neatly into the base and sides.

Spoon in half the chicken and pasta mixture. Make a large dip in the centre and fill with the meatballs and quail's eggs. Cover with the remaining chicken and pasta mixture. Dampen the edges of the pie crust with the beaten egg. Roll out the remaining pastry and use it to cover the top of the pie. Pinch the edges together, roughly trim, then twist the edges to form a sort of rope. Make a hole in the top and decorate as you like with the pastry trimmings (tassels are good!).

Mix the remaining beaten egg with the powdered saffron (if using) and brush all over the top of the pie. Bake in the preheated oven for 45 minutes–1 hour or until the pastry is golden. Allow to rest in the pan for 10 minutes before removing and carrying to the table.

SMOKED HAM, LEEK AND MUSHROOM PIE

When my sister had her first child some 18 years ago, a few days before Christmas, I made this pie for the family gathering on Boxing Day. I had travelled to London to see my new niece and help out as much as I could. I wanted us all to have a memorable Christmas despite all the trials and tribulations of new parenthood. The pie went down a storm and lasted for a couple of lunches as well. It's easy to prepare, eat and serve, and utterly delicious. Adding an extra egg yolk to the glaze will give a beautiful golden shiny crust. The pie can be made the day before and chilled, then re-glazed and cooked on the day you want to eat it.

2 quantities French Butter Pie Pastry (see page 29)

100 g/6½ tablespoons butter

450 g/1 lb. leeks, trimmed and finely sliced

100 g/scant 1 cup grated Gruyère cheese

50 g/⅔ cup grated Parmesan

225 g/8 oz. dark open-cup mushrooms, sliced

450 g/1 lb. oak-smoked cooked ham, diced

4 tablespoons wholegrain mustard

300 ml/1¼ cups fromage frais or crème fraîche

1 large egg, beaten with a pinch of salt, to glaze

salt and freshly ground black pepper

2 x 28 x 33-cm/11 x 13-inch baking sheets

holly leaf pastry cutters or templates (optional)

SERVES 12

First make the pastry following the instructions on page 29. When you get to step 9, divide the pastry into 2 pieces, approximately one-third and two-thirds, then shape into 2 thick rectangles. Wrap and chill for at least 30 minutes until firm.

When chilled, unwrap the smaller piece of pastry and roll out to fit the baking sheet, keeping any trimmings. Roll out the larger piece a little bigger (as this will cover the whole filled pie), slide onto another baking sheet (it will overhang a little so take care) and chill.

Preheat the oven to 200°C (400°F) Gas 6.

Prick the smaller pastry rectangle with a fork and bake in the preheated oven for 15 minutes, then leave to cool. Leave the oven on.

Remove the larger pastry rectangle from the fridge and allow to soften while you make the filling.

Melt the butter in a frying pan and add the leeks. Cook for a few minutes until beginning to soften, then stir in the Gruyère and Parmesan cheeses. Spread half this mixture over the cooked base, leaving a border around the edge.

Cover with half the sliced mushrooms, then the diced ham. Mix the mustard with the fromage frais and spread all over the ham. Season with pepper, then top with the remaining sliced mushrooms and leek mixture.

Moisten the edges of the cooked pastry base and cover with the larger sheet of pastry, pressing the edges down well to seal. Carefully trim the edges and brush the whole pie with the beaten egg. It will look like a flat cushion.

Re-roll the trimmings and cut out holly leaves (or something suitably Christmassy) with cutters or templates. Cover the whole pie with drifts of leaves, brushing with more of the beaten egg. Chill for 30 minutes, then bake in the oven, still at 200°C (400°F) Gas 6, for about 30 minutes until golden and crisp. Serve hot or cold, cut into squares.

FRENCH-CANADIAN TOURTIERE

A classic pie served at 'Le Réveillon', the Christmas Eve celebrations in French Canada. The pie was originally made from 'tourtes' (turtle doves or pigeons) and the dish in which it was made became known as a tourtière dish. Although made predominantly from minced pork nowadays, it can still contain a mix of game and family recipes are jealously guarded. Although this recipe uses pork, I often add minced venison or diced wild pigeon if I have it, and sometimes add chopped rosemary. The flavours in the pie develop even more the next day and it makes a fantastic lunch dish served with pickled gherkins and homemade red-cabbage coleslaw.

650 g/1½ lbs. lean medium minced/ground pork (not too fine)

1 onion, finely diced

1 garlic clove, crushed

1 teaspoon dried thyme

1 teaspoon dried sage

⅛ teaspoon ground cloves

1½ teaspoons celery salt

3 floury potatoes, peeled

1 quantity American Pie Crust (see page 30)

8–10 fresh sage leaves

salt and freshly ground black pepper

a 23-cm/9-inch, deep pie pan

SERVES 6

In a large mixing bowl, combine the pork, onion, garlic, thyme, sage, cloves and celery salt with 150 ml/⅔ cup water and at least ¼ teaspoon pepper. Tip this into a sauté pan and cook over medium heat, stirring now and then, for about 10 minutes until about half the water has evaporated and the pork is still pale but on no account brown. Turn the heat down to a simmer and cook for a further 30 minutes, stirring occasionally to prevent it sticking.

Meanwhile, boil the potatoes until tender, drain and roughly crush them. Mix them into the cooked pork and leave to cool.

Cut the pastry into 2 pieces, one piece slightly larger than the other. Roll out the larger piece on a lightly floured surface and use it to line the pie pan. Chill until firm.

Roll out the remaining pastry to a circle large enough to cover the pie with an overlap. Slide this onto a baking sheet and chill until needed (remove from the fridge 10 minutes before using).

Preheat the oven to 220°C (425°F) Gas 7 and set a heavy baking sheet on the middle shelf.

Spoon the cold meat mixture into the chilled pie crust and lay the fresh sage leaves all over the top of the meat.

Dampen the edges of the pastry with a little cold water, then lay the top crust over the pie. Press the edges to seal, then trim and flute to decorate. Slash the top crust so that the steam (and sage aroma) can escape.

Slide onto the baking sheet in the preheated oven and bake for 10 minutes, then reduce the temperature to 180°C (350°F) Gas 4 and bake for a further 30–40 minutes until golden brown. If the edges look like they are browning too much, cover them with strips of kitchen foil. Let cool for 10 minutes before slicing and serving.

COLD RAISED GAME PIE WITH RED ONION AND SLOE GIN MARMALADE

30 g/2 tablespoons butter

2 shallots, chopped

1 garlic clove, crushed

4 tablespoons peaty Scotch malt whisky

150 ml/⅔ cup reduced game stock or consommé

10 juniper berries, crushed

600 g/1 lb. 5 oz. venison shoulder, minced/ground

300 g/10½ oz. pork belly, minced/ground

1 tablespoon dried thyme

1–2 teaspoons mixed/apple pie spice

2 tablespoons marmalade

1–2 tablespoons green peppercorns in brine, drained

200 g/7 oz. cubed pancetta (finely diced) or dry-cure streaky bacon

350 g/12 oz. venison fillet or strip loin, cubed and chilled

1 quantity French Butter Pie Pastry (see page 29)

1 egg, beaten, to glaze

salt and freshly ground black pepper

FOR THE RED ONION AND SLOE GIN MARMALADE:

100 g/6 tablespoons unsalted butter

675 g/1½ lbs. red onions, thinly sliced

1½ teaspoons salt

1 teaspoon ground black pepper

100 g/½ cup caster/granulated sugar

6 tablespoons sherry vinegar

3 tablespoons sloe gin

2–3 tablespoons redcurrant jelly

240 ml/scant 1 cup red wine

a 1.5-litre/quart raised pie mould

SERVES 8

A magnificent centrepiece for a posh picnic. Any mix of seasonal game will do — wild boar, hare, rabbit, pheasant, grouse, partridge or wild pigeon. Cut the meat large enough to be evident when layering up and make sure the colours and flavours are evenly distributed. Starting a couple of days ahead will simplify the assembly.

Preheat the oven to 190°C (375°F) Gas 5.

Melt the butter in a saucepan, add the shallots and garlic and cook for 5 minutes until soft. Stir in the whisky, game stock and half the crushed juniper berries. Boil hard to reduce by half, then strain through a sieve/strainer into a small bowl and leave to cool.

Mix the minced/ground venison and pork with the thyme, mixed/apple pie spice, remaining crushed juniper berries, marmalade and 1½ teaspoons salt. Lightly crush the peppercorns and add to the mix. Beat the reserved strained stock into the meat mix, then fold in the cubed pancetta. Cover and chill.

On a lightly floured surface, roll out two-thirds of the pastry to a manageable thickness and use it to line the pie mould, pressing well into all the nooks and crannies and making sure you have an overhang of pastry over the top edge.

Press a thin layer of the minced meat mixture over the bottom of the mould and cover with a layer of cubed venison. Season well. Add another layer of minced meat and press down well. Repeat until all the meat is used up, ending with a layer of minced meat.

Roll out the remaining pastry for the lid. Brush the edges of the pie with the beaten egg and cover with the pastry lid. Press to seal, trim and crimp the edges. Use the remaining pastry to cut out decorations and attach to the top of the pie with beaten egg. Brush the entire top with more egg, set in a baking pan and bake in the preheated oven for 15 minutes to set the pastry. Reduce the oven to 150°C (300°F) Gas 2 and cook for a further 1¾ hours. Remove from the oven, let cool for 20 minutes, then ease out of the mould. Leave to cool, then chill. Bring to room temperature before serving.

To make the onion marmalade, heat the butter in a saucepan until just turning golden. Add the onions, salt, pepper and sugar. Stir, cover the pan and cook gently, for about 20 minutes, stirring occasionally, until the onions are softened and have turned moist brown. Add the vinegar, sloe gin, redcurrant jelly and wine. Cook, uncovered, for a further 30 minutes. Let cool, then pot and store in the fridge. Serve warm or at room temperature with slices of the pie.

TIP: A raised pie mould is usually a metal pan made of 3 parts — a base and 2 sides — clipped or hinged together to help unmould the pie. Extravagant in shape and usually quite tall in stature, the classic one has a 'nipped-in' waist.

ROAST SMOKED SALMON KOULIBIACA

I have been very fortunate to collaborate with Rosie Campbell-Preston of Inverawe Smokehouses over the past ten years. We have created some delicious smoked fish recipes together, this being a favourite. Roast smoked salmon is brined salmon, suspended over hot smoke, which cooks and smokes it at the same time. Serve in generous slices with a mixed-leaf salad tossed in a sharp lemony dressing.

75 g/5 tablespoons butter

6 spring onions/scallions, chopped

125 g/4½ oz. button mushrooms, roughly chopped

75 g/⅓ cup basmati rice

225 ml/scant 1 cup light fish stock

600 g/1 lb. 5 oz. roast smoked salmon (or smoked salmon)

2 large eggs, hard-boiled and peeled

1–2 tablespoons chopped fresh dill

3 tablespoons chopped fresh parsley

finely grated zest and freshly squeezed juice of ½ lemon

1 recipe Rough Puff Pastry (see page 25) or Cheat's Puff Pastry (see page 27)

1 egg, lightly beaten

salt and freshly ground black pepper

a heavy baking sheet, greased with butter

SERVES 4–6

Melt the butter in a saucepan set over medium heat, add the spring onions/scallions and mushrooms and cook for 2–3 minutes. Stir in the rice and mix well, then pour in the fish stock. Bring to the boil, then turn the heat down to low, cover and simmer for 12 minutes. Remove from the heat, uncover and leave to cool.

Break the roast smoked salmon into large flakes (or roughly chop the smoked salmon) and place in a mixing bowl. Roughly chop the hard-boiled eggs and add to the salmon with half the dill and half the parsley, mixing well. Taste and season, but don't use too much salt as the salmon will be salty.

Tip the cooked rice into another bowl and use a fork to fluff it up, then mix in the remaining dill and parsley and the lemon zest and juice. Taste and season.

Roll out the pastry to a 35 x 27-cm/14 x 11-inch rectangle directly onto a piece of clingfilm/plastic wrap. Spoon half the rice mix onto the centre of the pastry, widthways leaving a good bit of pastry at either side that will eventually wrap over the filling. Leave a border of at least 2.5 cm/1 inch at either end.

Carefully spoon the salmon mix evenly over the rice, piling it high. You may want to use your hands to mould this into shape. Top with the remaining rice mix, pressing and moulding it into a rounded loaf shape.

Bring one side of the pastry up and over the filling, brush the edge with beaten egg, then bring the other side over to enclose the filling completely. Pinch the ends to seal. Using the clingfilm/plastic wrap, carefully flip over onto the prepared baking sheet so that the sealed edges are underneath. Brush the surface of the pastry all over with the beaten egg. (If it is a special occasion, use extra pastry to cut into fish shapes to decorate, then glaze again. Alternatively, glaze first, then use the tip of a teaspoon to indent half-moons to resemble fish scales.) Chill for at least 30 minutes.

Preheat the oven to 220°C (425°F) Gas 7.

Bake in the preheated oven for 20–25 minutes or until deep golden brown. Remove from the oven and leave it to rest for about 10 minutes before slicing and serving.

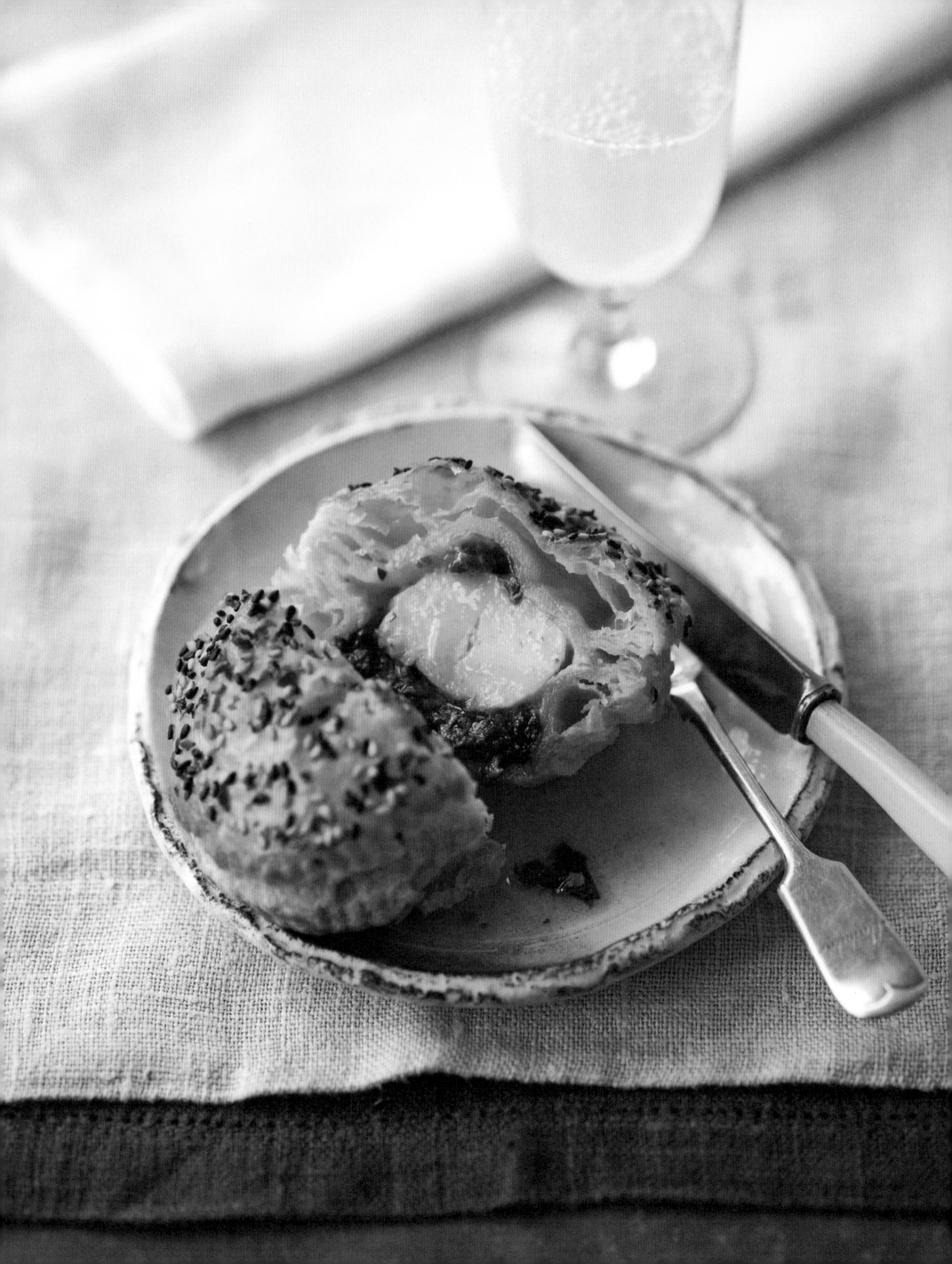

SCALLOP AND BLACK PUDDING PUFFS

The scallops should be about the same width as the sliced black pudding. If you cannot find the smaller size of black pudding, slice a larger one and, using a pastry cutter, stamp out rounds to fit. The pastry recipe makes a lot, so freeze any remaining pastry for up to three months. Serve as a starter with a baby-leaf salad.

6 medium-sized fresh scallops, removed from the shell

freshly squeezed juice of 1 lemon

1 quantity Rough Puff Pastry (see page 25) or Cheat's Puff Pastry (see page 27)

6 x 1-cm/½-inch slices cut from a small 170 g/6 oz. black pudding

1 egg, beaten with a pinch of salt, to glaze

Furikake seasoning (Japanese seaweed and sesame seasoning)

salt and freshly ground black pepper

FOR THE BASIL AND SUN-DRIED TOMATO BUTTER:

175 g/1½ sticks unsalted butter, soft

3 tablespoons finely shredded fresh basil

6 sun-dried tomatoes in oil, drained and finely sliced

2 tablespoons grated Parmesan

a 6-hole bun pan

a 12-cm/5-inch round pastry cutter

a 10-cm/4-inch round pastry cutter

a 10-cm/4-inch round fluted pastry cutter

MAKES 6

First, make the flavoured butter. Beat the butter until really soft, then beat in the basil, tomatoes, Parmesan and seasoning. Spoon onto a sheet of clingfilm/plastic wrap and roll up into a log by twisting the ends. Chill for at least an hour until hard.

Preheat the oven to 220°C (425°F) Gas 7.

Remove the roe (if any) from the scallops and discard or freeze. Pull off the little hard muscle found on the scallop opposite the roe and remove any membrane. Put the scallops into a bowl, season with salt and pepper and toss with the lemon juice.

On a lightly floured surface, roll out the puff pastry to rectangles measuring approximately 35 x 27 cm/14 x 11 inches. Using the large round cutter, stamp out 6 rounds from one rectangle and use them to line the bun-pan holes. Use the smaller plain cutter to stamp out 6 rounds from the other rectangle for the tops and set aside.

Cut 12 slices of flavoured butter from the roll. Lay a slice of black pudding in the base of each pie and top with a slice of butter, then with a whole scallop and then with another slice of butter. Dampen the edges with the beaten egg, then top with the remaining pastry rounds and seal.

Trim by using the small fluted cutter to stamp over each pie, being careful that they are still well sealed. Make a tiny steam hole in the top of each puff, brush with beaten egg and sprinkle with the Furikake seasoning. Bake in the preheated oven for 10–13 minutes until puffed and golden. Serve immediately.

TIP: If you can't find black pudding, this recipe would also work with chorizo sausage. Furikake seasoning is available from larger supermarkets, some Asian supermarkets and online.

GOATS' CHEESE, MUSHROOM AND ROSEMARY PITHIVIERS

Golden puff pastry filled with goat's cheese, sliced mushrooms and walnuts, and marked in a particular pattern, sort of like a Catherine wheel, typical of a Pithiviers: this would make any vegetarian feel special. Either make one large one for a crowd, or several smaller individual ones. I serve this with a generous spoonful of confit of baby plum tomatoes and basil. Heat some olive oil, add the whole tomatoes and season. Slam on a lid and cook until the tomatoes just begin to collapse but not disintegrate. Stir in shredded basil, taste and season. Heavenly!

5 tablespoons extra virgin olive oil

2 garlic cloves, roughly chopped

1 tablespoon chopped fresh rosemary

300 g/10 oz. large dark open-cup mushrooms, thickly sliced

350 g/12 oz. leeks, trimmed and sliced

2 quantities Rough Puff Pastry (see page 25) or Cheat's Puff Pastry (see page 27)

50 g/⅓ cup walnuts, chopped (not too finely)

200 g/7 oz. any type of goats' cheese, crumbled

1 small egg, plus 1 egg yolk, to glaze

salt and freshly ground black pepper

a 27-cm/11-inch dinner plate

SERVES 6

Put 3 tablespoons of the olive oil and the garlic and rosemary into a spice grinder and blitz until smooth. Tip into a sauté pan and add the mushrooms. Stir to coat, add 2 tablespoons water, salt and pepper and cook over medium heat for about 5 minutes until soft and all the liquid has disappeared. Spread out on a tray and let cool.

Heat the remaining oil in the sauté pan and sauté the leeks for about 5 minutes until soft. Season and leave to cool.

On a lightly floured surface, roll out one quantity of the pastry to a rough circle that is just bigger than the dinner plate. Using the plate as a guide, cut out a circle around the plate with a sharp knife. Slide the pastry circle onto a heavy baking sheet.

Spoon the cooled leeks onto the pastry circle in an even layer, leaving a 2.5-cm/1-inch bare rim of pastry all round. Mix the mushrooms gently with the walnuts and goats' cheese and spoon evenly over the leeks. Lightly flatten the top, keeping the pastry edges clean. Brush the pastry edge with the beaten egg.

Roll out the second quantity of pastry into a rough circle a good bit larger than the plate (it must be big enough to drape over the filling comfortably). Using a rolling pin, lift it up and lay over the filling, unrolling as you go. Gently mould it around the filling and press down around the edge to seal. Trim the edge to a width of 2.5 cm/1 inch. Now knock up the pastry edges (see page 16) and scallop them. Brush all over with the beaten egg and chill for at least 30 minutes.

Preheat the oven to its hottest setting.

Once chilled, use the tip of a small sharp knife or scalpel to lightly score a wheel pattern on the surface of the pastry, being careful not to cut through the pastry. (The pie can be kept chilled like this overnight, ready to cook the next day.)

Bake the pie in the preheated oven for 10 minutes, then reduce the temperature to 220°C (425°F) Gas 7 and cook for a further 20–25 minutes until crisp and golden brown (lay a sheet of kitchen foil on top if it is browning too quickly). Remove from the oven and allow to rest for 5 minutes before serving with tomato confit.

ROASTED MEDITERRANEAN VEGETABLE PIE

I had the idea for this pie when making a roasted vegetable terrine in Sicily. Roasting vegetables brings out all their natural sweetness and concentrates the flavours, and packing them in a pastry case just makes them even better! Not just for vegetarians...

1 quantity French Butter Pie Pastry (see page 29)

2–3 aubergines/eggplant

3 large red bell peppers

2 red onions

100 ml/6½ tablespoons olive oil

1 courgette/zucchini, sliced

250 g/9 oz. baby plum tomatoes

2 teaspoons dried oregano

50 g/⅔ cup grated Parmesan

75 g/1½ cups fine fresh white breadcrumbs

2 garlic cloves, grated

1 generous tablespoon finely chopped basil

2–3 tablespoons double/heavy cream, mixed with a pinch of salt, to glaze

salt and freshly ground black pepper

2 large roasting pans

a 900-g/2-lb. loaf pan (approx. 23 cm/9 inches long x 10 cm/4 inches wide x 7.5 cm/3 inches deep), well greased with butter

SERVES 4

Preheat the oven to 200°C (400°F) Gas 6 and set a heavy baking sheet on the lower middle shelf.

Cut off one quarter of the pastry, wrap in clingfilm/plastic wrap and reserve for the lid. Roll out the remaining pastry on a lightly floured surface and use to line the loaf pan, making sure the pastry slightly drapes over the top. Chill until needed.

Cut the aubergines/eggplant into 1.25-cm/½-inch cubes and transfer to a large bowl of heavily salted water. Set a plate on top to keep the cubes submerged and leave for 30 minutes.

Halve the peppers lengthways, remove all the white membrane and seeds and place in a roasting pan. Drizzle with half the olive oil. Slice the onions into thick rounds and add these to the same pan, spreading them out in one layer. Spoon over the olive oil gathered in the pan and put in the preheated oven to roast for about 20 minutes.

Meanwhile, drain the aubergines/eggplant and pat dry with paper towels. Tip into the other roasting pan, drizzle with the remaining oil and season. Roast in the oven for 10 minutes, then stir, move to one side and add the courgettes/zucchini to the pan. Sprinkle with a teaspoon of dried oregano. Return to the oven to roast for another 10 minutes and remove the peppers and onions, which should be tender by now. Peel the skin from the peppers, return to the pan and let cool, then drain and reserve the juices from the pan.

When the aubergines/eggplant and courgettes/zucchini are ready they will be slightly brown on their edges. Remove from the oven, drain off the juices and reserve. Set aside to cool. Leave the oven on.

Mix the Parmesan, breadcrumbs, garlic, basil and the remaining teaspoon of oregano together, cover and set aside.

Now the choice is yours – you can mix the cooked vegetables with the tomatoes, then combine with the breadcrumb mix, pile into the chilled pastry-lined pan and lightly press down. Alternatively, arrange all the vegetables in layers, sprinkling with the breadcrumb mix between each layer.

Moisten the pastry edges with cream. Roll out the reserved lid pastry and lay on top of the pie. Press the edges together to seal and trim with a sharp knife. Flute or scallop the edges, if wished. Use the trimmings to decorate the top of the pie and brush with the cream glaze. Make steam holes all over the top of the pie using a fork.

Bake in the preheated oven for 10 minutes then reduce the heat to 180°C (350°F) Gas 4 and bake for a further 25–30 minutes or until the pastry is set and golden. Remove from the oven and leave to stand for 10 minutes before removing from the pan to serve. Delicious eaten warm or cold.

PORTABLE
PIES

PIGGY PIES

When we were kids, Mum would make these pies (without quail's eggs) for a special treat if we were going to the beach for the day. The water was so cold on the East Coast of Scotland that we were very glad of a good rub down with a rough towel and a pie in the hand! In those days we would never have seen a quail's egg – now they are in most supermarkets. We would have loved them – baby eggs!

12 quail's eggs

225 g/8 oz. lean minced/ground pork

100 g/3½ oz. dry-cure bacon or pancetta, minced/ground or finely chopped

1 small onion, grated

3 tablespoons Branston Pickle, or similar

2 teaspoons dried mixed herbs

4 tablespoons chopped fresh parsley

1 quantity Basic Shortcrust Pastry (see page 22)

1 egg, beaten with a pinch of salt, to glaze

salt and freshly ground black pepper

a 9-cm/3½-inch round pastry cutter

a 7-cm/2¾-inch round pastry cutter

a 12-hole muffin pan

MAKES 12

Prick through the shell at the wide end of each quail's egg with a pin – this will allow the trapped air to escape and prevent the eggs cracking as they cook. Soft-boil the eggs in a pan of boiling water for 2 minutes 45 seconds. Drain, then cool under running water until completely cold. Carefully peel off the shells under cold running water and keep submerged in a bowl of cold water until ready to use.

Preheat the oven to 400°F (200°C) Gas 6.

To make the filling, put the minced/ground pork, bacon or pancetta, onion, pickle, dried herbs and parsley in a large mixing bowl. Mix using your hands or a wooden spoon and season with a little salt and plenty of pepper.

Roll out the pastry on a lightly floured surface to a thickness of about 3–4 mm/⅛ inch. Cut 12 rounds using the large pastry cutter, and 12 rounds for the lids using the smaller pastry cutter.

Carefully press and mould the larger rounds into the holes of the muffin pan, making sure they reach the top. Half-fill each with the pork filling, top with a quail's egg, then top with another layer of filling, carefully tucking it around the egg.

Brush the inside edges of each filled pie with a little beaten egg and place a lid on top, pressing the edges together to seal. Trim if necessary. Make a hole in the top of each pie (I use the tip of a metal piping nozzle/tip), brush the tops with more beaten egg and bake in the preheated oven for 20 minutes. Reduce the oven temperature to 160°C (325°F) Gas 3 and cook for a further 25–30 minutes until the pastry is golden and the filling is cooked through. Cool on a wire rack, then wrap in greaseproof/baking paper and store in the fridge for up to 5 days.

BACON, EGG AND PARSLEY PIE

This is the British equivalent of a French Quiche Lorraine, but with a double crust. The crust keeps the filling from drying out, and the addition of the parsley is a must – it gives it a wonderful pale green colour and a delicate flavour! It is traditional to layer up the bacon with the egg mix, but I think it is easier to eat if the bacon is chopped. Using organic eggs will normally give the filling a richer, darker colour. This is perfect for picnics, lunch boxes or a simple lunch served with a peppery watercress salad.

1 quantity Basic Shortcrust Pastry (see page 22)

4 large eggs, plus 2 egg yolks

300 ml/1¼ cups double/heavy cream or crème fraîche

3 tablespoons roughly chopped fresh parsley

a pinch of ground mace or freshly grated nutmeg

250 g/9 oz. smoked dry-cure, rindless streaky bacon, roughly chopped

1 egg, beaten, to glaze

freshly ground black pepper

a 20-cm/8-inch pie plate or loose-based cake pan

SERVES 4–6

Roll out two-thirds of the pastry on a lightly floured surface and use it to line the pie plate or cake pan. Roll out the remaining pastry to a round that will easily cover the pie and slide it onto a baking sheet. Chill both the lined pie plate and the lid pastry for at least 20 minutes.

Preheat the oven to 220°C (425°F) Gas 7 and set a heavy baking sheet on the middle shelf.

Put the whole eggs, egg yolks, cream, parsley and mace or nutmeg into a blender or liquidizer and blend until smooth and a lovely pale green colour. Alternatively, use a stick/immersion blender.

Scatter the bacon over the base of the pastry and pour over the cream mixture. Brush the edges of the pastry with the beaten egg and lay the pastry lid over the pie. Seal the edges together well, trim and crimp if you like. Brush the surface with beaten egg, and make a couple of steam holes in the top of the pie. Decorate the top with pastry trimmings if you like – a porky pig or two is fun!

Bake in the preheated oven for 15 minutes to set the pastry, then reduce the oven temperature to 180°C (350°F) Gas 4 and bake for a further 45 minutes or until golden in colour and set. Remove from the oven and cool for 10 minutes before removing from the pan to cool on a wire rack. Serve warm or at room temperature.

VEAL AND HAM PIE WITH SAGE AND CAPERS

This is the quintessential raised pie – one that Ratty and Mole from *The Wind in the Willows* would have packed in a wicker hamper and taken on their picnic, drifting down the river. The filling uses a shoulder cut, which is full of flavour and keeps very moist during cooking, and the savoury jelly locks in those flavours and keeps the pie nice and succulent. The salted capers and sage are a must – don't leave them out!

2 quantities Rich Hot-water Crust (see page 31)

FOR THE FILLING :

375 g/13 oz. boneless shoulder of pork, trimmed and cut into small cubes

300 g/10½ oz. boneless shoulder of veal, trimmed and cut into small cubes

2 tablespoons chopped fresh sage

2 tablespoon salted capers, rinsed and chopped

1 teaspoon anchovy essence

¼ teaspoon ground mace or freshly grated nutmeg

1 egg, beaten

salt and freshly ground black pepper

FOR THE JELLY :

285 ml/9½ oz. canned chicken consommé

2 level teaspoons powdered gelatine

an 18-cm/7-inch springform pan, 6 cm/2½ inches deep, well greased with butter

a small funnel

SERVES 4

Combine all the ingredients for the filling in a large mixing bowl, season well with salt and pepper, cover and set aside.

Cut off one-third of the dough, cover and set aside. On a lightly floured surface, roll out the remaining pastry to a circle about 30 cm/12 inches in diameter. Lift the pastry into the pan and press gently to mould evenly over the base and sides. Chill for 20 minutes.

Spoon the filling into the chilled, lined pan, pressing it down well with the back of the spoon.

Roll out the remaining dough to a circle just larger than the pan diameter. Brush the edges of the dough in the pan with cold water, cover with the lid and press the edges together firmly to seal. Trim off the excess dough and make a hole in the centre of the pie. Use the pastry trimmings to decorate the pie to your liking and brush the top of the pie with beaten egg. Chill for 30 minutes. Meanwhile, preheat the oven to 200°C (400°F) Gas 6.

Sit the pie on a baking sheet and bake in the centre of the preheated oven for 30 minutes. Reduce the oven temperature to 180°C (350°F) Gas 4 and bake for a further hour, covering with kitchen foil if the pastry starts to over-brown. Take the pie from the oven, leave to stand for 5 minutes, then carefully remove the side of the pan.

Brush the sides of the pie liberally with more beaten egg and return it to the oven for a further 20 minutes until the sides are golden brown (keep the top of the pie covered with kitchen foil). Remove from the oven and transfer the pie, still on its base, to a wire rack to cool completely.

To make the jelly, put 3 tablespoons of the consommé into a small saucepan and sprinkle the gelatine powder on top. Leave to stand for 2–3 minutes to 'sponge', then heat gently until the gelatine has dissolved. Stir into the remaining stock and let cool until slightly syrupy. Using a small funnel inserted into the hole in the centre, pour the jelly into the pie until the pie will take no more. Chill overnight before serving.

DORIS TIDDY'S PASTIES

The ultimate Cornish Pastie as taught to me by the amazing Doris Tiddy of St Mawes, Cornwall. She made the very best pasties (or 'paaahrstie' as she called them) I have ever tasted. We used to dream of them all year from one summer to the next when we would make the long journey from Scotland to Cornwall for our summer holidays. Doris and her husband Ron always invited us to tea – and what a spread! The epicentre of which was a pile of golden pasties. Nirvana!

Start by making the pastry. Sift the flour with the salt into a large mixing bowl. Rub in the butter, then cut in the lard using a round-bladed knife, leaving large pieces of lard big enough to see. Add 3 tablespoons of the water and mix to bind. You may like to add more water if it's looking a bit dry. Knead once only – the pastry should look quite streaky and lumpy. Gather into a ball, then cut into four equal pieces.

On a lightly floured surface, roll out each piece to a thickness of 1.25 cm/½ inch – no less! Use the dinner plate as a guide to cut out 2 rounds from each piece of pastry, making 8 in all.

Preheat the oven to 220°C (425°F) Gas 7.

Dice the beef as finely as you can without mincing it and set aside.

Divide two-thirds of the onion equally between the pastry rounds, leaving a good edge to seal the pastry together. Top with the potato, then season with salt and pepper and add 3 sprigs of parsley to each pasty. Scatter over the meat, season with pepper, then add the turnip and season with salt and pepper again. Finally, scatter over the remaining onion.

Dampen the pastry edges with beaten egg and draw up over the filling to meet either over the top or at the side. Press the edges to seal, fold over, then crimp roughly. Set the pasties onto the heavy baking sheets and brush all over with beaten egg, to glaze. Make a small hole in the top of each one and bake in the preheated oven for 15 minutes to set the pastry. Reduce the oven temperature to 180°C (350°F) Gas 4 and bake for a further 30 minutes or until deeply golden. Serve hot, warm or cold for a picnic, wrapped in a paper napkin.

FOR THE PASTIE PASTRY:

450 g/3½ cups plain/all-purpose flour

½ teaspoon salt, or more (Doris insisted that you use a lot of salt)

45 g/3 tablespoons butter, chilled and diced

115 g/4 oz. pure lard, chilled and diced

3–4 tablespoons ice-cold water

FOR THE FILLING:

900 g/2 lbs. beef skirt steak, trimmed

225 g/8 oz. onion, finely diced

225 g/8 oz. potato, finely diced

fresh parsley sprigs (3 per pastie)

225 g/8 oz. turnip or swede/rutabaga, finely diced

1 egg, beaten, to glaze

salt and freshly ground black pepper

a 25-cm/10-inch dinner plate

2 heavy baking sheets

MAKES 8

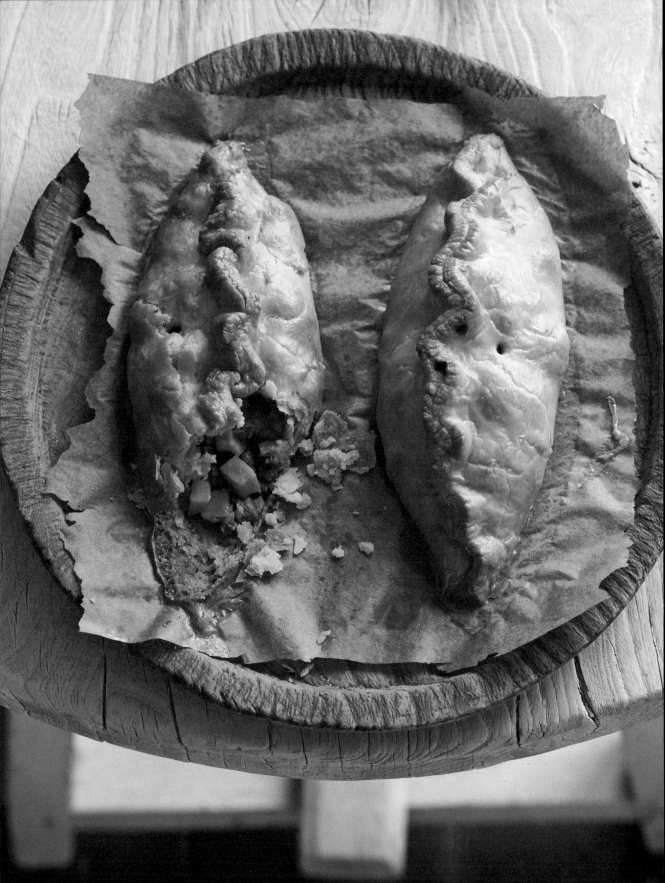

CORNED BEEF AND SWEET POTATO PASTIES

These pasties are almost like corned beef hash in pastry. I use orange-fleshed sweet potatoes, which I find have a lovely smooth texture and rich, sweet earthy taste and contrast nicely with the saltiness of the corned beef. The fresh thyme is essential, and lemon thyme is even better. Be sure to season with plenty of black pepper. These are perfect picnic or packed lunch fodder and mini ones make fantastic, homely canapés.

2 quantities Basic Shortcrust Pastry (see page 22)

2 tablespoons sunflower oil

1 onion, finely chopped

1 large orange-fleshed sweet potato, diced

2 tablespoons spicy mango chutney or sweet chilli sauce

2 tablespoons chopped fresh thyme or lemon thyme

450 g/1 lb. canned corned beef, chilled and diced

1 egg, beaten, to glaze

salt and freshly ground black pepper

a 20-cm/8-inch dinner plate

a baking sheet lined with non-stick baking parchment

MAKES 6 LARGE PASTIES OR 12 SMALLER ONES

Roll out the pastry on a lightly floured surface and cut out 6 rounds, using the plate as a guide.

Heat the oil in a sauté pan and add the onion. Cook over medium heat for 5 minutes until beginning to soften. Add the sweet potato and cook, stirring from time to time, for 10 minutes or until just tender. Stir in the chutney or sweet chilli sauce and thyme and leave to cool. Once cold, fold in the corned beef and season well.

Divide the mixture between the 6 pastry circles and crimp the edges together to seal in the filling – over the top or to the side, the choice is yours! Brush with the beaten egg and chill for 30 minutes.

Preheat the oven to 200°C (400°F) Gas 6.

Arrange the chilled pasties on the prepared baking sheet, make a little steam hole in each one and bake in the preheated oven for 20–30 minutes until the pastry is golden brown. Remove from the oven and serve hot or transfer to a wire rack to cool.

KEEMA BRIDIES

The infamous Scottish hand-held pie, originating in Forfar, is given the curry treatment here, thus marrying two cultures that have sat side by side in Scotland since immigrant workers from Pakistan and India came to work in the flax and jute mills. They were responsible for introducing to Scotland what was to become our other national dish… the curry. I have combined Indian and Pakistani spicing and traditional Scottish pie-making to make an irresistible combination. These are just wonderful eaten in a steamy car on a miserable rainy day when you have pulled into a layby because you couldn't find a picnic spot – very comforting!

FOR THE TRADITIONAL BRIDIE PASTRY:

250 g/2 cups strong white bread flour

75 g/⅔ cup plain/all-purpose flour

½ teaspoon salt

175 g/1½ sticks unsalted butter, chilled and diced

3 tablespoons ice-cold water

FOR THE MEAT FILLING:

3 tablespoons vegetable suet/ shortening

1 onion, very finely chopped

a good squeeze of garlic purée

a good squeeze of ginger purée

3 teaspoons coriander seeds

2 teaspoons cumin seeds

a pinch of ground cinnamon

a pinch of ground cloves

½ teaspoon garam masala

600 g/1 lb. 5 oz. trimmed shoulder of lamb or shin of beef, coarsely minced/ground

50 g/½ cup frozen peas

2 tablespoons chopped fresh coriander/cilantro

salt and freshly ground black pepper

a baking sheet, greased with butter

MAKES 4

For the pastry, sift the flours and salt into a food processor. Add the butter and process until it is just incorporated. Add just enough of the water to bind to a stiff dough in a couple of quick pulses. Tip out onto a lightly floured surface and knead lightly into a ball, then flatten and wrap in clingfilm/plastic wrap. Chill for at least 1 hour.

For the filling, melt the suet/shortening in a saucepan set over medium heat. Add the onion, garlic and ginger purées and spices, and cook for 5 minutes. Put the minced/ground meat into a large mixing bowl and add the spiced onion mixture along with the peas and coriander/cilantro. Season with plenty of salt and pepper and fork through lightly.

Divide the chilled pastry into 4 and roll out each piece to a large long oval. Spoon the filling onto the top half of each pastry oval, dividing equally between the 4 bridies and leaving a border around the edges. Dampen the edges, then fold the other half of the pastry over the filling to enclose it. Trim the edges into a neat horseshoe shape and press down firmly to seal, then crimp all the way around to give a neat finished look. (According to Sue Lawrence, Scottish food writer, this technique is known as 'dunting and nicking'.) Using a sharp knife, make a small elongated hole in the top of each bridie to allow the steam to escape.

Place the bridies on the prepared baking sheet and chill for at least an hour before baking. (They are not generally glazed with anything.) Meanwhile, preheat the oven to 200°C (400°F) Gas 6.

Bake the bridies in the preheated oven for 35–40 minutes or until golden brown. Serve warm, not hot.

5-SPICED VENISON PUFFS

I first tasted these delectable pastries in Yauatcha in London's Soho. I was having a celebratory meal with my friends who are venison dealers and, once tasted, we just couldn't get enough of these little pastries. This is my guess as to how they are made with my own additions, although I suspect there is a secret recipe for the incredible pastry!

1 recipe Rough Puff Pastry (see page 25) or Cheat's Puff Pastry (see page 27)

2 tablespoons runny honey

2 egg yolks, beaten

2–3 tablespoons toasted sesame seeds

FOR THE VENISON FILLING:

2 tablespoons sunflower or rapeseed oil

350 g/12 oz. minced/ground or finely diced lean venison

1 small onion, finely chopped

1 small carrot or parsnip, grated

1 teaspoon cornflour/cornstarch

200 ml/¾ cup oyster sauce

1 teaspoon soft light brown sugar

2 teaspoons sesame oil

½ teaspoon Chinese 5-spice powder

salt and freshly ground black pepper

an 8-cm/3-inch round pastry cutter

a large baking sheet lined with non-stick baking parchment

MAKES 12

To make the venison filling, heat the sunflower oil in a frying pan set over medium heat and stir-fry the venison for a couple of minutes until beginning to brown, breaking up any lumps as you fry. Add the onion and carrot and fry for 2–3 minutes, then stir in the cornflour/cornstarch, oyster sauce, brown sugar, sesame oil, 5-spice powder and ¼ teaspoon each of salt and pepper. Mix well, then remove from the heat and leave to cool.

Preheat the oven to 190°C (375°F) Gas 5.

On a lightly floured surface, roll out the pastry to a thickness of 3–5 mm/⅛–¼ inch. Using the pastry cutter, stamp out 12 circles of pastry. Remove and discard the trimmings.

Hold a circle of pastry in the palm of your hand and spoon a level tablespoon of venison filling into the centre. Using your index fingers and thumbs, gently bring the pastry upwards around the filling, but not over it, and pinch it together into a triangle shape. Arrange the puffs on the prepared baking sheet, folds upwards, and bake in the preheated oven for 3 minutes.

In a small bowl, mix together the honey and 1 tablespoon cold water to make a runny syrup.

Remove the puffs from the oven and turn the baking sheet around, then return to the oven for 3 minutes. Remove from the oven again, brush the tops of the puffs with the beaten egg yolk, and return to the oven for a further 1 minute to set the glaze. Finally, lift out of the oven and brush with a little honey syrup, sprinkle with the sesame seeds and return to the oven for 20–30 seconds to set the syrup and finish the cooking. Remove from the oven and serve immediately or serve cold at a posh picnic!

CHORIZO AND BLACK OLIVE SAUSAGE ROLLS

Sausage rolls are the most popular snack you can ever offer. Everyone just loves them, especially served warm straight out of the oven – but they also make a fantastic gourmet lunch box treat. If fresh chorizo sausage is difficult to find, use a good garlicky butcher's sausage and mix in 1–2 teaspoons of sweet or hot Spanish pimentón (smoked paprika) and a couple of tablespoons of red wine.

400 g/14 oz. fresh cooking chorizo sausages (not the harder salami type)

2 tablespoons chopped fresh parsley or coriander/cilantro

25 g/3 tablespoons minced red onion or shallot

2 tablespoons roughly chopped black olives

1 quantity Basic Shortcrust Pastry (see page 22)

1 egg, beaten

a little warm milk mixed with a pinch of powdered saffron, to glaze

salt and freshly ground black pepper

a baking sheet lined with non-stick baking parchment

MAKES 12

Preheat the oven to 200°C (400°F) Gas 6.

Squeeze the chorizo sausages out of their skins and into a large mixing bowl. Add the parsley, red onion and olives and season with salt and pepper. Using your hands, mix and squeeze the mixture until well combined.

Roll out the pastry on a lightly floured surface to a large rectangle about 2–3 mm/¹⁄₁₆ inch thick, and cut in half lengthways to make 2 rectangles. With floured hands, roll the meat mixture into two long sausages the same length as the pastry and place one down the centre of each piece.

Dampen the pastry along one long edge of each rectangle, then bring the dry pastry up and over the sausagemeat, followed by the dampened side, pressing the edges together. Flip each roll over, making sure that the join is underneath the roll.

Combine the beaten egg with the saffron-infused milk and brush over the rolls carefully, then cut into 5-cm/2-inch lengths. Either prick each one with a skewer a few times, or snip a couple of small 'V's in the pastry with a pair of scissors. (This allows steam to escape during cooking and stops the pastry from over-puffing up.) Arrange on the prepared baking sheet and bake in the preheated oven for 25–30 minutes until set and golden. Serve warm.

TIP: These can be frozen in their raw state and cooked from frozen – just cook them for 5–10 minutes longer.

CRAB EMPANADAS

I love making these little pies with our local, sweet fresh crabmeat in the summer. I have tried making them with frozen crabmeat, but it really is too wet and hasn't the same intense flavour – at a pinch, use canned crabmeat. Crab marries well with chilli, and I use the bottled sweet and sour Peppadew peppers from South Africa. They are mild enough not to dominate and are a beautiful red colour. If you go to the trouble of making puff pastry, you will have enough for two batches – freeze one half of the pastry for later.

175 g/6 oz. fresh white crabmeat

6 spring onions/scallions, chopped

3 Peppadew peppers, finely diced or minced

2 tablespoons sour cream or crème fraîche, plus 1–2 tablespoons extra, to glaze (optional)

a dash of Green Jalapeno Tabasco sauce, plus extra, to glaze (optional)

1 quantity Rough Puff Pastry (see page 25)

1 tablespoon black onion seeds (kalonji), to sprinkle (optional)

salt and freshly ground black pepper

an 8-cm/3-inch round pastry cutter

a baking sheet lined with non-stick baking parchment

MAKES 10

Preheat the oven to 400°C (200°F) Gas 6.

Mix the crabmeat, spring onions/scallions, diced peppers, sour cream and the Tabasco sauce in a medium-sized bowl, then taste and season with salt and pepper. Set aside.

On a lightly floured surface, roll out the pastry to a thickness of 3–5 mm/⅛–¼ inch. Using the pastry cutter, stamp out 10 circles of pastry. Remove and discard the trimmings.

Place teaspoons of the crab mixture into the centre of each pastry circle, dampen the edges with a little water and fold each in half. Pinch the edges to seal, then use a fork or the end of a spoon to make a decorative edge. Arrange the empanadas about 5 cm/ 2 inches apart on the prepared baking sheet.

The empanadas can be left unglazed for a matt finish, or at this point can be brushed with 1–2 tablespoons of sour cream mixed with 2 teaspoons water, a pinch of salt and a dash of Tabasco. Very lightly sprinkle with black onion seeds (if using).

It is better to bake these immediately as the mixture is quite wet and could make the pastry go soggy. Bake in the preheated oven for about 12 minutes until puffed and golden. Eat warm or cold.

SPICY VEGETABLE SAMOSAS

These are wonderful served warm, fresh out of the fryer, or equally good eaten cold from a lunch box. Any root vegetable can be used in the filling, as long as it is cooked until really tender before filling the samosa. I sometimes use whole spices, such as coriander and fennel seeds, cumin and curry leaves instead of curry paste for a more authentic taste. They can be reheated in a hot oven for 5 minutes. Cucumber raita makes the perfect accompaniment for dipping.

2 tablespoons ghee or vegetable oil

1 small onion, diced

2 garlic cloves, crushed

1 tablespoon chopped fresh ginger

1–2 teaspoons of your favourite curry paste

2 teaspoons black mustard seeds

200 g/7 oz. floury potatoes, diced

1 small orange-fleshed sweet potato, diced

1 tablespoon palm sugar or soft brown sugar

80 g/⅔ cup frozen peas

50 g/⅓ cup roasted cashew nuts, chopped

25 g/½ cup roughly chopped fresh coriander/cilantro

2 quantities Basic Shortcrust Pastry (see page 22)

vegetable oil, for deep-frying

salt and freshly ground black pepper

a 12-cm/5-inch round pastry cutter

MAKES ABOUT 20

Heat the ghee or oil in a large heavy-based non-stick frying pan set over medium heat. Cook the onion, garlic and ginger with the curry paste and mustard seeds for 5 minutes, stirring regularly until golden and smelling really good.

Add the potato, sweet potato and sugar. Cook, stirring regularly, for 8–10 minutes or until the potatoes are tender. Stir in the peas, reduce the heat to low, cover and steam for a further 3 minutes. Remove from the heat and let cool, then taste and season and stir in the cashews and coriander/cilantro.

Roll out the pastry on a lightly floured surface. Using the pastry cutter, cut 20 circles from the pastry. Place 1 generous tablespoon of filling in the middle of each circle. Brush the edges lightly with water to dampen, then fold the pastry over and pinch the sides together to seal firmly.

Heat the oil in a deep-fat fryer or stable wok to 170°C (325°F), or until a cube of bread browns in 20 seconds. Deep-fry 3 samosas at a time for about 3–4 minutes, turning over halfway through and cooking until crisp and golden and the pastry has bubbled a little. Drain on paper towels and keep warm while you fry the remainder. Serve warm or cold.

GREEK SPINACH, FETA AND OREGANO FILO PIE

The first time I ate this was on holiday in Greece when I was a student. There was a little island off the coastline where we were camped and the owners of the campsite arranged a day trip to it, complete with picnic. This was one of the simple but delicious components that we unpacked, still sitting in its baking dish. It was fantastic, redolent with the aroma of dried wild oregano. Ricotta or even English Wensleydale will work well if you are not partial to salty feta.

2 tablespoons Greek olive oil

1 bunch of spring onions/scallions, finely sliced

2 garlic cloves, crushed

450 g/1 lb. young spinach leaves, washed

4 large eggs, beaten

200 g/7 oz. Greek feta cheese, crumbled

1 teaspoon freeze-dried oregano

a large pinch of freshly grated nutmeg

finely grated zest of 1 lemon

4 large sheets of thin Greek-style filo/phyllo pastry (about 225 g/8 oz.)

75 g/5 tablespoons butter, melted

salt and freshly ground black pepper

a 25 x 20-cm/10 x 8-inch baking pan

SERVES 6

Preheat the oven to 190°C (375°F) Gas Mark 5.

Heat the oil in a large saucepan, add the spring onions/scallions and garlic and sauté for 2 minutes. Pile in the spinach, cover with a lid and cook for 3 minutes over a high heat or until the leaves are just wilted. Tip into a sieve/strainer and press out the excess moisture. Transfer to a large mixing bowl and stir in the eggs, feta, oregano, nutmeg, lemon zest, a little salt and plenty of pepper, mixing well.

Brush the inside of the baking pan with melted butter. Carefully brush the filo/phyllo pastry sheets all over with melted butter.

Lay the first sheet of pastry in the pan, pressing it into the base and up the sides. Place the second sheet on top at 90 degrees, making sure the pastry will overhang the pan. Repeat with the remaining 2 sheets of pastry.

Spoon the filling into the pastry-lined pan and level. Fold over the overlapping pastry, brushing with more butter as necessary. Brush the top with the remaining butter.

Bake in the preheated oven for 50–60 minutes until the pastry is golden brown and crisp. Remove from the oven and cover with a clean dish towel for 5 minutes to lightly soften the pastry before you mark it. With a sharp knife, mark the pie into 6 squares and leave to cool. Serve warm or cold.

TIP: For a neater look to the top of the pie, use only 3½ sheets of the filo/phyllo pastry to line the pan, saving a half sheet to lay over the top and neaten the look. Brush with butter before baking.

SWEET PIES

BUTTERED CIDER APPLE DOUBLE-CRUST PIE

Cider, apples and butter with a hint of tangerine – what could be better? Grating the cooking apples makes a softer filling, which really melts in the mouth and is so easy to prepare. Dessert apples don't work as well – they are too sharp and won't collapse to a creaminess as tarter cooking apples (Bramleys) do. Serve with custard or cream.

1 quantity Basic Shortcrust Pastry (see page 22)

2 large cooking apples, peeled, cored and roughly grated

finely grated zest and freshly squeezed juice of 1 tangerine, or similar

75 g/5 tablespoons golden caster/natural cane sugar, plus 2 tablespoons for dredging

75 g/5 tablespoons butter, melted

2 tablespoons apple cider, apple brandy or Calvados

1 egg, beaten

a 20-cm/8-inch (inside measurement) pie plate with a 2.5-cm/1-inch rim

a pie funnel

blossom pastry cutters (optional)

SERVES 4

Preheat the oven to 200°C (400°F) Gas 6 and set a heavy baking sheet on the middle shelf.

Roll out half the pastry on a lightly floured surface and use to line the pie plate. Set a pie funnel in the middle of the pie plate.

Put the grated apple in a mixing bowl and add the tangerine zest and juice, sugar, 50 g/4 tablespoons of the melted butter (keep the remainder warm), the cider or brandy and the beaten egg. Mix well and spoon into the lined pie plate, levelling the surface.

Roll out the remaining pastry to a round slightly larger than the pie plate. Cut out a long strip of pastry about 2.5 cm/1 inch wide and use it to line the rim of the dish, then brush with a little water. Make a hole in the middle of the remaining pastry and, using a rolling pin, lift it up and drape over the pie plate, making sure that the hole drops over the pie funnel. Trim off the excess pastry and knock up the edges (see page 16). If desired, use pastry cutters to cut shapes from any excess pastry and use them to decorate the top of the pie.

Set the pie on the baking sheet in the preheated oven and bake for 15 minutes. Reduce the temperature to 190°C (375°F) Gas 5 and bake for a further 15 minutes to set the pastry. Remove from the oven and brush with the remaining melted butter, dredge with the 2 tablespoons of sugar and return to the oven for a further 10–15 minutes until golden brown and crusty – watch closely as it may brown quite quickly.

DEEP-DISH TOFFEE APPLE PIE

I can never resist a homemade apple pie – it is my downfall! To make matters worse (or better!) I add smashed-up toffees to the apples that melt into the pie while it cooks, cloaking the apples in caramel. Cutting through the sugary crust into the golden apples releases a tantalizing toffee apple aroma. Mixing dessert apples with a proportion of cooking apples sharpens the flavour. Serve with clotted cream or ice cream or, better still, pour cream into the pie through the steam hole just before serving!

75 g/3 oz. hard toffees

1 kg/2¼ lbs. dessert apples (such as Cox's, Russet, McIntosh or Macoun), peeled, cored and thickly sliced

finely grated zest and freshly squeezed juice of 1 small lemon

3 cloves

½ teaspoon mixed/apple pie spice (or cinnamon if you prefer)

1 quantity Basic Shortcrust Pastry (see page 22)

1 tablespoon each plain/all-purpose flour and caster/granulated sugar, mixed, plus extra caster/granulated sugar for dredging

1 small egg white

a 23-cm/9-inch pie plate

SERVES 6

Preheat the oven to 200°C (400°F) Gas 6.

Put the toffees in a plastic bag and use a rolling pin to smash them into small pieces. Add them to a large mixing bowl with the apples, lemon juice and zest, cloves and mixed spice/apple pie spice.

Divide the pastry into 2 pieces and, on a lightly floured surface, roll out each piece to a circle that will easily cover the pie plate. Line the plate with one of the pastry circles and sprinkle the base with the flour and sugar mix. Spoon the apple mixture into the pie plate and mound up in the centre. Brush the pastry edges with a little water and cover the pie dish with the remaining pastry circle, sealing and crimping the edges. Cut off any excess pastry and use the trimmings to cut shapes to decorate the pie, if you have time. Make a slit through the pastry on top to allow the steam to escape while cooking.

Beat the egg white to a loose froth and brush evenly all over the pie, then dredge generously with sugar. Set the pie on a baking sheet and bake in the preheated oven for about 35–40 minutes until golden and firm with a sugary crust.

TIP: Sometimes when I have run out of mixed/apple pie spice, I use real Chinese 5-spice powder – without garlic and onion additions!

SPICED BAKED APPLE PIES

I used to adore apple dumplings as a child – apples stuffed with dried fruit and spice, all wrapped up in a golden crust. They are a little fiddly to make and can burst open in the oven, so I have developed these little darlings with a bay leaf and a sliver of cinnamon acting as a stalk to remind us of what is buried under the pastry! Needless to say, serve these with your finest egg and vanilla custard.

80 g/⅔ cup mixed sultanas/golden raisins and chopped dried figs

3 tablespoons dark or golden rum

30 g/2½ tablespoons soft light brown sugar

½ teaspoon mixed/apple pie spice

125 g/1 stick softened butter, plus extra for spreading

6 eating apples, peeled and cored

1 quantity Basic Shortcrust Pastry (see page 22)

6 small bay leaves

6 thin shards of cinnamon stick

6 round individual ovenproof dishes (see recipe for size)

SERVES 6

Put the sultanas/golden raisins and figs into a screw-top jar with the rum, shake and leave to soak for at least 2 hours or overnight (shaking occasionally). Once soaked, mix with the sugar, mixed/apple pie spice and butter. Spoon the spiced fruit and butter mixture into the holes in the cored apples, pressing in with the handle of a teaspoon. Spread a little more butter over the apples. Carefully place each apple into a round dish or ramekin in which they fit snugly, protrude above the top edge, but don't touch the sides.

Roll out the pastry and cut out 6 circles a good bit larger than the diameter of the dishes. Brush the rims of the dishes with a little water and set a circle of pastry on top of each dish, gently moulding over each apple. Press the edges of the pastry to the rim to seal and make a tiny steam hole in the top of each pie. Use any pastry trimmings to cut shapes to decorate the top of the pies, then chill for 20 minutes. Meanwhile, preheat the oven to 200°C (400°F) Gas 6.

Set the pies on a baking sheet and bake in the preheated oven for 15 minutes to set the pastry. Reduce the temperature to 150°C (300°F) Gas 2 and stick a bay leaf and cinnamon shard into the steam holes, then bake for a further 40 minutes until the apples are soft but not collapsing. (If they look like they are browning too much, cover with kitchen foil.)

MUM'S MINCE PIES

My mother has always made these for Christmas – they are my absolute favourite type of mince pie: pastry on the bottom, and a sort of melting piped shortbread on top of the mincemeat. She keeps them frozen, to pop into the oven at a moment's notice, so that they are really fresh. They are filled with her own mincemeat of course, but you can buy excellent ready-made stuff now. This is about the only time I am forced to use a piping bag with any enthusiasm!

1 quantity Rich Shortcrust Pastry
(see page 24)

225 g/2 sticks unsalted butter, soft

50 g/⅓ cup icing/confectioners'
sugar, sifted

1 teaspoon pure vanilla extract

225 g/1¾ cups plain/
all-purpose flour

250–300 g/9–10½ oz. luxury
mincemeat

a 7.5-cm/3-inch fluted pastry cutter

a 12-hole bun pan

*a piping bag fitted with a star
nozzle/tip*

MAKES 12

On a lightly floured surface, roll out the pastry thinly and cut out 12 rounds using the pastry cutter. Line the bun pan with the pastry, pressing the rounds into the holes. Prick the bases and chill or freeze for 15 minutes.

Meanwhile, make the Viennese paste. In a large mixing bowl and using an electric hand-whisk, cream the butter with the icing/confectioners' sugar and vanilla. It must be very, very pale, soft and light or it will not pipe. Gradually work in the flour, a tablespoon at a time, beating well between each addition. Spoon into the piping bag. (Keep this at warm room temperature or it will not pipe.)

Fill the tartlets with the mincemeat, then pipe a swirl of Viennese paste on top of each pie. Chill in the fridge for 30 minutes.

Preheat the oven to 180°C (350°F) Gas 4.

Bake the pies in the preheated oven for about 20 minutes until a pale golden brown. Let cool in the pan, then transfer to a wire rack and dust with icing/confectioners' sugar to serve. Serve warm or at room temperature – never cold!

LATTICE-TOPPED CHERRY PIE

I think this is one of my favourite pies of all – it is so simple and is best made with luscious Morello cherries picked straight off the tree – summer baked in a pie! I have fond memories of tucking into a similar pie as a child when visiting friends in their cottage by the sea. Vera had baked this pie for us coming, and as all the adults seemed more interested in chatting and drinking, I began to work my way through that pie until it was almost gone… sorry, Vera, but it was that good! This is in memory of Vera – a wonderful cook and generous hostess. Serve with cream or vanilla ice cream.

FOR THE AMERICAN CREAM CHEESE PASTRY:

300 g/2⅓ cups plain/all-purpose flour

2 tablespoons icing/confectioners' sugar

a large pinch of salt

175 g/1½ sticks unsalted butter, chilled and diced

175 g/¾ cup Philadelphia cream cheese

4–6 tablespoons milk, chilled, plus extra to glaze

FOR THE CHERRY FILLING:

3 x 350-g/12-oz. packs frozen pitted Morello cherries (or 1 kg/2¼ lbs., drained weight, canned Morello cherries)

200 g/1 cup caster/granulated sugar, plus extra for sprinkling

½ teaspoon ground cinnamon or a good pinch of allspice

freshly squeezed juice of 1 lemon

5 tablespoons cornflour/cornstarch

a 23-cm/9-inch metal or enamel pie plate

a baking sheet lined with non-stick baking parchment

SERVES 6

For the pastry, sift the flour into a large mixing bowl with the icing/confectioners' sugar and salt. Rub in the butter and cream cheese until the mixture resembles coarse breadcrumbs. Add enough of the milk to mix to a soft dough. Gather up the dough to form a ball and knead very briefly until smooth. Divide into 2 pieces, then wrap and chill both portions in the fridge for at least 1 hour.

For the filling, mix the cherries with all the remaining ingredients and leave to stand for 20 minutes, then stir once more.

Preheat the oven to 220°C (425°F) Gas 7.

On a lightly floured surface, roll out half the pastry and use it to line the pie plate. Roll out the second half of the dough to a rectangle and cut into wide strips long enough to drape over the pie. Put the strips onto the prepared baking sheet and chill until needed.

Spoon the cherries into the lined pie plate, mounding them up in the centre. Brush the edges of the pastry with water, then lay the pastry strips on top, weaving them to form a lattice. Trim the edges, then crimp to seal. Brush the top with milk and sprinkle with sugar.

Set the pie on a baking sheet to catch any juices and bake in the preheated oven for 20 minutes to set the pastry. Reduce the oven temperature to 180°C (350°F) Gas 4 and bake for a further 30–40 minutes until the thickened cherry juices bubble up through the lattice. Cover the top loosely with kitchen foil if the pastry looks as if it is browning too quickly. Serve warm or cold.

TIP: This pie is very juicy – you may want to keep some juices back and boil separately to thicken them.

TROPICAL TREACLE TART

This is a very creamy variation of treacle tart, using real black treacle, rich dark rum and lime to flavour a coconut custard. Rum has such an affinity with all these ingredients — because they all come from the same part of the world, perhaps! Using coconut milk with the coconut adds more flavour, but you could use whole milk instead. Serve with a good dollop of the rum cream.

Preheat the oven to 200°C (400°F) Gas 6.

Roll out the pastry as thinly as you can on a lightly floured surface and use it to line the tart pan. Prick the base of the pastry with a fork, line with baking parchment or kitchen foil, then fill with baking beans and bake blind for 15 minutes. Remove the parchment or foil and beans and return to the oven for a further 5–8 minutes to dry out the pastry. Remove from the oven and leave to cool.

Meanwhile, in a large mixing bowl, whisk the coconut milk with the rum, black treacle, eggs and the lime zest and juice. Reserve 3 tablespoons of the coconut for decoration and add the remaining coconut to the mixing bowl. Stir well, then pour the mixture into a saucepan and stir over a medium heat for about 5 minutes until beginning to thicken. Do not let this boil or it will curdle.

Set the cooled pie crust (still in the pan) on a baking sheet and pour in the filling. Return to the oven for 25 minutes until just set and a little puffy.

To make the rum cream, whisk the dark rum, cream and icing/confectioners' sugar together until holding soft peaks. Transfer to a bowl, cover and chill until needed.

When the tart is cooked, remove from the oven and leave to stand for 5 minutes, then sprinkle with the reserved coconut (or you could just dust with more icing/confectioners' sugar).

Serve warm (not hot) or cold with the rum cream.

½ quantity Basic Shortcrust Pastry (see page 22), made with all butter

200 ml/¾ cup coconut milk

3 tablespoons dark rum

70 g/¼ cup plus 1 tablespoon black treacle or molasses

2 eggs

finely grated zest and freshly squeezed juice of 1 lime

125 g/1¾ cups sweetened tenderized coconut

FOR THE RUM CREAM :

3 tablespoons dark rum

300 ml/1¼ cups double/heavy cream

3 tablespoons soft light brown sugar

a 20.5-cm/8-inch loose-based tart pan, 4 cm/1½ inches deep

SERVES 4-6

FRESH DATE AND GINGER CREAM PIE

Medjool dates give a rich fudgey sweetness to this creamy custard tart. Considered the jewel in the crown of all Middle Eastern dates, they are plump, moist, very sweet and have a generous amount of flesh around a relatively small pit. They are available in many larger supermarkets and health food shops. Dates have been used in British cooking since the Middle Ages, and pies just like this would have been made at that time – especially as it contains the much prized spice, ginger in all its forms. If a real date lover, then double the amount of dates and halve the custard.

½ quantity American Pie Crust (see page 30), made with 1 teaspoon ground ginger sifted with the flour

250 g/9 oz. fresh Medjool dates

2 balls stem ginger in syrup, drained and finely chopped

2 tablespoons brandy (optional)

350 ml/1⅓ cups sour cream

125 g/½ cup plus 1 tablespoon golden caster/natural cane sugar

2 tablespoons cornflour/cornstarch

2.5-cm/1-inch piece fresh ginger, grated

⅛ teaspoon ground ginger

3 large eggs, beaten

2 teaspoons pure vanilla extract

a pinch of salt

a 23-cm/9-inch pie plate

SERVES 8

Roll out the pastry on a lightly floured surface and use it to line the pie plate. Trim off any excess pastry and use it to cut shapes to decorate the edge of the pie. Prick the base with a fork and and chill for at least 30 minutes.

Preheat the oven to 200°C (400°F) Gas 6 and set a heavy baking sheet on the middle shelf.

Slit each date along its length and flick out the pit. Keep them whole and fill each one with a little of the chopped stem ginger, then sprinkle with the brandy (if using). Arrange the dates over the base of the pie crust, open edge uppermost.

In a large mixing bowl, whisk together the sour cream, sugar, cornflour/cornstarch, fresh and ground gingers, beaten eggs, vanilla and salt. Pour this over the dates, being careful not to dislodge them.

Place the pie on the baking sheet in the preheated oven and bake for 10 minutes. Reduce the oven temperature to 180°C (350°F) Gas 4 and bake for a further 30 minutes or until the centre is set.

Remove the pie to wire rack and leave to cool. Serve slightly warm or cold, just as it is.

SHOOFLY PIE

This intriguingly named American Amish classic gets its name (I am told) from the label of the brand of molasses that published the original recipe – Shoo Fly Molasses. Molasses, being sweet and sticky, would attract flies that would have to be shooed away! The filling is black and sticky with a soft, pale, powdery crumb topping. This could be the closest US equivalent to the British Treacle Tart. It is rich and utterly delicious, and perfect served with whipped cream.

1 quantity American Pie Crust (see page 30), made with half white cooking fat/shortening, half butter

FOR THE CRUMB TOPPING:

165 g/1⅓ cups plain/all-purpose flour

125 g/⅔ cup packed soft dark brown sugar

50 g/4 tablespoons unsalted butter, chilled and cubed

¼ teaspoon salt

FOR THE MOLASSES FILLING:

¾ teaspoon bicarbonate of soda/baking soda

175 ml/¾ cup boiling water

225 g/scant 1 cup black treacle or molasses

1 large egg, beaten

1 teaspoon pure vanilla extract

a 23-cm/9-inch metal pie plate

SERVES 8–10

Roll out the pastry on a lightly floured surface and use it to line the pie plate. Trim off the excess pastry and prick the base with a fork. Chill for 30 minutes.

Preheat the oven to 200°C (400°F) Gas 6 and set a heavy baking sheet on the middle shelf.

Line the chilled pie crust with baking parchment or kitchen foil, then fill with baking beans. Set the pie plate on the baking sheet in the prehated oven and bake blind for 15 minutes. Remove the parchment or foil and beans and return to the oven for a further 8–10 minutes to dry out the pastry. Remove from the oven, place on a wire rack and leave to cool completely.

Reduce the oven temperature to 180°C (350°F) Gas 4.

To make the crumb topping, put the flour, sugar, butter and salt into a food processor and process until it forms fairly fine crumbs (don't overprocess). Reserve 6 tablespoons and set both aside.

To make the filling, sprinkle the bicarbonate of soda/baking soda into a mixing bowl and pour the boiling water over it. Pour in the treacle or molasses, beaten egg and vanilla extract and whisk well with a balloon whisk to combine. Stir in the larger amount of crumbs and whisk again. Pour into the cooled pie crust and sprinkle the remaining 6 tablespoons of crumb mixture evenly over the top.

Gently set the pie on the baking sheet in the preheated oven and bake for 40–45 minutes or until the filling just begins to puff up and crack slightly. Remove from the oven and transfer to a wire rack to cool completely before serving. The filling should still be slightly moist and sticky in the centre.

PUMPKIN PIE

My Scottish-Canadian cousin Deirdre introduced us to this when living with us for a while in Scotland back in the 1960s. Unimaginable now, but it was so exotic to us, having never even seen an American pumpkin (the Scots made turnip or swede lanterns at Halloween). We had a wonderful shop nearby – known as an 'Italian Warehouseman' – and there we found imported cans of pumpkin purée. It has remained a family favourite ever since. Butternut squash purée makes an ideal substitute and gives a brighter colour to the filling.

1 quantity Basic Shortcrust Pastry (see page 22)

475-g/15-oz. can pumpkin purée or 500 ml/2 cups of homemade (see below)

100 g/½ cup packed soft light brown sugar

3 eggs

200 ml/¾ cup evaporated milk or double/heavy cream

120 ml/½ cup golden syrup/light corn syrup or light molasses

a good pinch of salt

1 teaspoon ground cinnamon

½ teaspoon mixed/apple pie spice

1 teaspoon pure vanilla extract

2 tablespoons golden or spiced rum (optional)

a 20.5-cm/8-inch metal or enamel pie plate

a maple leaf pastry cutter (optional)

SERVES 4-6

Preheat the oven to 190°C (375°F) Gas 5.

Roll out the pastry thinly on a lightly floured surface and use it to line the pie plate, trimming off the excess pastry. Either crimp the edge of the pastry or use the pastry trimmings to cut leaves to decorate the edge. Prick the base all over with a fork, then line with baking parchment or kitchen foil and baking beans and bake blind for 12–15 minutes. Remove the foil and beans and return to the oven for a further 5 minutes to dry out the pastry. Leave to cool.

Reduce the oven temperature to 160°C (325°F) Gas 3.

Place all the remaining ingredients in a food processor and process until smooth. Set the cooled pie crust on a baking sheet and pour in the filling. Bake in the preheated oven for about 1 hour or until just set. If the pastry edges are beginning to brown too much before the filling is set, cover the edges with kitchen foil before returning to the oven. Remove from the oven to a wire rack and leave to cool in the pie plate. Serve warm or at room temperature, not chilled.

TIP: If you can't find cans of pumpkin or butternut squash purée, you can prepare your own. Cut 750 g/1½ lbs. of unpeeled pumpkin or squash into large chunks and bake in an oven preheated to 160°C (325°F) Gas 3 for about 1 hour. Alternatively, cook the chunks of pumpkin in the microwave in a covered heatproof bowl. (Boiling it won't work as it will make the pumpkin too wet.) When cooled, scrape the flesh from the skin and purée in a food processor.

SOURED CREAM RAISIN PIE

This is almost like a very light cheesecake baked in a double crust – very rich and luscious. I have used rich shortcrust for this with great success. Serve it with extra whole raisins plumped up in sweetened rum overnight. This is always best served cold as it will be too soft to cut if warm.

1 quantity American Pie Crust (see page 30)

150 g/1 cup large juicy raisins, chopped

3 tablespoons spiced rum, warm

2 large eggs

225 g/1 cup plus 2 tablespoons caster/superfine sugar

250 ml/1 cup sour cream

1 tablespoon freshly squeezed lemon juice

¼ teaspoon freshly grated nutmeg

a good pinch of salt

2–3 tablespoons demerara sugar, for dredging

a 23-cm/9-inch metal pie plate

SERVES 4–6

Preheat the oven to 230°C (450°F) Gas 8 and set a heavy baking sheet on the middle shelf.

Divide the pastry dough into 2 pieces. Roll one half out on a lightly floured surface and use it to line the pie plate. Trim off the excess pastry.

Soak the chopped raisins in the rum for about an hour until the rum is absorbed.

Using an electric hand whisk, whisk the eggs with the caster/superfine sugar until the mixture is pale and mousse-like. Set aside.

Reserve 2 tablespoons of the sour cream for the glaze. Whip the remaining sour cream with the lemon juice, nutmeg and salt until slightly thickened. Carefully fold into the egg mixture, then fold in the soaked chopped raisins. Spoon into the pie crust.

Roll out the remaining pastry thinly so that it will cover the top of the pie. Brush the edges of the pie with a little water, pick up the pastry on the rolling pin and lift it over the pie to cover it. Fold the top crust carefully under the lower crust and press the edges together to seal. Brush with the reserved sour cream and dredge with the demerara. Slash the top a couple of times to allow the steam to escape. Place the pie on the baking sheet in the preheated oven and bake for 10 minutes. Reduce the oven temperature to 180°C (350°F) Gas 4 and bake for a further 20 minutes until the pastry is set and pale coloured. Leave to cool before serving.

DOUBLE CRANBERRY AND ORANGE PIE

This is the sort of pie you see in Western films, sitting enticingly on the window sill in a log cabin with a view out over the prairie, while a brave pioneer mom puts the coffee on to brew on the range and sets the table with a gingham cloth – although it is usually apple pie! The popped cranberries glisten through the lattice top and stain the pastry with bubbling juices. I mix in dried cranberries to absorb some of the liquid and add texture. Serve warm with a scoop of vanilla ice cream on top or even better – a scoop of orange sorbet.

1 quantity American Pie Crust (see page 30)

300 g/3 cups fresh or unthawed frozen cranberries

100 g/¾ cup dried cranberries

100 g/½ cup caster/superfine sugar, plus extra for dredging

3 tablespoons golden syrup/light corn syrup

finely grated zest and freshly squeezed juice of 1 tangerine

3 tablespoons orange liqueur

30 g/2 tablespoons butter

a little milk, for brushing

a 23-cm/9-inch metal pie plate

a baking sheet lined with non-stick baking parchment

SERVES 6–8

Cut the pastry into 2 pieces, one slightly larger than the other. Roll out the larger piece to a circle just larger than the pie plate and the smaller piece to a rectangle measuring about 25 x 8 cm/10 x 3 inches. Use the circle to line the pie plate but do not trim the edges yet. Slip the pastry rectangle onto the prepared baking sheet and cut eight lattice strips about 1 cm/½ inch wide using a sharp knife. Chill both the pie crust and lattice strips in the fridge for 30 minutes.

Preheat oven to 220°C (425°F) Gas 7.

Put the fresh and dried cranberries into a mixing bowl, add the sugar, syrup, tangerine zest and juice and orange liqueur and stir to mix well. Tip the mixture into the chilled pie crust and dot with the butter. Dampen the rim of the pastry and arrange the lattice strips across the pie in a star shape, almost marking out the portions, pressing down the ends firmly to seal. Trim off the excess pastry and crimp the edges. Brush the pastry with milk and dredge heavily with more sugar.

Set the pie on a baking sheet and bake in the preheated oven for 15 minutes. Reduce the oven temperature to 180°C (350°F) Gas 4 and bake for a further 30–40 minutes until the pastry is golden brown and the juices bubbling all over.

MISSISSIPPI MUD PIE

A dream of a pie for any chocolate lover. The filling puffs up, then settles down and cracks as it cools to resemble the cracked and dried riverbed, but the centre is soft and velvety. For those who like chocolate and peanut butter, and are not allergic, whisk a couple of generous tablespoons into the filling as it melts in the saucepan – delicious! I sometimes decorate this with 'rocks' of chocolate-covered cinder toffee. Serve with whipped or pouring cream, or scoops of coffee ice cream.

1 quantity American Pie Crust (see page 30)

75 g/5 tablespoons unsalted butter

50 g/1¾ oz. dark/bittersweet chocolate, chopped

6 tablespoons unsweetened cocoa powder, sifted

3 large eggs

250 g/1¼ cups caster/granulated sugar

2 tablespoons crème fraîche or sour cream

3 tablespoons golden syrup/light corn syrup

2 teaspoons pure vanilla extract

chocolate shavings, chocolate-covered nuts or chocolate buttons, to decorate

a 23-cm/9-inch loose-based pie plate, 3.5 cm/1½ inches deep

SERVES 8

Roll out the pastry on a lightly floured surface and use to line the pie plate. Chill for 30 minutes.

Preheat the oven to 180°C (350°F) Gas 4 and set a heavy baking sheet on the middle shelf.

For the filling, melt the butter in a small saucepan. Remove from the heat and add the chocolate and cocoa powder, stirring until the chocolate is melted and the mixture is smooth. Set aside.

Whisk the eggs and sugar together until the mixture is pale and creamy, then whisk in the crème fraîche or sour cream, syrup and vanilla extract. Fold this light mixture into the chocolate mix and pour into the pie crust.

Set the pie on the baking sheet in the preheated oven and bake for 35–40 minutes or until the filling puffs up, cracks and forms a crust on top (but is still a bit wobbly in the centre). Remove from the oven and cool for 30 minutes on a wire rack.

Chill for at least 2 hours before serving decorated with chocolate shavings, chocolate-covered nuts or chocolate buttons to look like the twigs and pebbles on a riverbed.

TIP: This can be made 2 days in advance and stored in the fridge.

JACK D'S PECAN PIE

Pecan pie is one of my personal favourites, especially when laced with a good slug of Jack Daniel's. The secret of this pie is not to overcook it or it will be too set and dry. I have made this successfully by substituting maple syrup for the treacle or molasses – it just tastes sweeter. A squeeze of lemon juice in the filling will bring out the flavour of the nuts. Although this looks spectacular as a large pie, it makes lovely little individual pies for a dinner party. Serve with whipped cream or ice cream.

½ quantity American Pie Crust (see page 30)

350 g/12 oz. (2¾ cups) pecan nut halves

4 large eggs

300 ml/1¼ cups black treacle or molasses

55 g/4 tablespoons butter, melted

4 tablespoons Jack Daniel's whiskey

2 tablespoons plain/all-purpose flour

½ teaspoon ground nutmeg

¼ teaspoon salt

a 23-cm/9-inch metal pie plate

SERVES 6–8

Preheat oven to 200°C (400°F) Gas 6.

Roll out the pastry on a lightly floured surface and use it to line the pie plate, then chill for 30 minutes. Prick the base all over with a fork, then line with baking parchment or kitchen foil and baking beans and bake in the preheated oven for 15 minutes. Remove the foil and beans and return to the oven for a further 10 minutes to dry out the pastry. Leave to cool.

Reduce the oven temperature to 180°C (350°C) Gas 4.

Chop half the pecan halves finely, reserving the remaining half for decoration.

In a large mixing bowl, whisk the eggs lightly until pale and frothy. Whisk in the treacle or molasses, melted butter and whiskey. Stir in the flour, nutmeg and salt.

Scatter the chopped nuts evenly over the pastry base, then pour in the treacle mix and level the surface.

Arrange the remaining pecan halves over the surface of the pie in concentric circles, starting at the centre and working outwards.

Set the pie on a baking sheet and bake in the preheated oven for 35–45 minutes or until the pastry is golden and the filling is just set in the middle. Cool for up to 15 minutes before serving as the filling will be very hot. Serve warm or at room temperature.

PECAN AND MAPLE SYRUP BAKLAVA

Baklava has always been a favourite of mine and I love to serve this deep-flavoured version with strong hot sweet Turkish coffee – if that's all too sweet for you, then serve with a good Italian double espresso. To make the filling moister, you can mix some of the maple syrup with the butter and use this to brush between the layers. Acacia or orange blossom honey is a good alternative to the maple syrup.

150 g/10 tablespoons unsalted butter, melted

250 g/2 cups pecan nuts

50 g/¼ cup soft light brown sugar

¼ teaspoon mixed/apple pie spice (or more if you like spice)

100 g/¾ cup shelled pistachio nuts, roughly chopped

450 g/1 lb. large, thin Greek-style filo/phyllo pastry sheets

175 g/¾ cup pure maple syrup, warm

18 x 28-cm/7 x 11-inch shallow baking pan

MAKES 12–20 SQUARES

Preheat the oven to 220°C (425°F) Gas 7. Brush the baking pan with some of the melted butter.

Grind the pecans with the sugar and mixed/apple pie spice in a food processor. Mix with the chopped pistachio nuts.

Unroll the pastry and trim to make 25-cm/10-inch squares. Place one half on top of the other and cover with clingfilm/plastic wrap to prevent it drying out. Place one sheet of filo/phyllo in the pan, allowing it to come up the sides. Brush with melted butter. Repeat with 5 more pastry sheets. Sprinkle with 50 g/⅓ cup of the nut mixture. Repeat this 4 more times, giving 5 layers of nut mixture. Top with 5 more sheets of pastry, brushing with butter as you go. Trim to fit the pan.

Mark the surface into 12–20 squares with the tip of a very sharp knife. Bake in the preheated oven for 15 minutes. Reduce the oven temperature to 180°C (350°F) Gas 4 and bake for a further 10–15 minutes until golden. Remove from the oven and spoon the warmed maple syrup over the baklava. Leave to cool in the pan for about 2 hours to absorb the syrup and soften slightly. Cut the marked squares with a sharp knife and serve.

KEY LIME PIE

A classic pie from the Florida Keys, where this recipe has been popular since the late 19th century. Some are topped with cream, others meringue. Whichever way you like it, choose juicy fresh limes that are heavy for their size and never make this with bottled lime juice!

Preheat the oven to 190°C (375°F) Gas 5.

Put the biscuits/cookies and crackers in a plastic bag and bash with a rolling pin until finely crushed.

Melt the butter in a saucepan, then mix in the biscuit/cookie crumbs and sugar until well coated. Spread the crumb mixture evenly over the base and up the sides of the tart pan, pressing in lightly with the back of a spoon (or a potato masher). Set on a baking sheet with a lip to catch any melting butter that may escape. Bake in the preheated oven for 8–10 minutes, then remove from the oven and let cool. Leave the oven on.

Using an electric hand whisk, beat the egg yolks and lime zest together for about 5 minutes until pale, thick and fluffy. Gradually whisk in the condensed milk and continue to whisk for a further 5 minutes until very thick and fluffy. Now whisk in the lime juice, spoonful by spoonful, keeping the mix nice and fluffy (it will thin down a bit).

Pour the filling into the cooled baked pie crust and set the pan on a baking sheet. Bake in the centre of the oven for about 15 minutes or until just set but still a bit wobbly in the centre. Transfer to a wire rack to cool for 30 minutes, cover and refrigerate for at least 2 hours.

To serve, whip the cream with the icing/confectioners' sugar until thick but spreadable (do not overwhip). Spread or pipe the cream over the top of the pie and decorate with slices of lime. Alternatively, you can just decorate with lime slices and serve with dollops of whipped cream on the side.

TIP: This freezes well for up to 3 months, minus the cream.

FOR THE PIE CRUST:

200 g/7 oz. mixed ginger nuts and digestives/gingersnaps and graham crackers

100 g/6½ tablespoons unsalted butter

50 g/¼ cup caster/granulated sugar

FOR THE KEY LIME FILLING:

3 large egg yolks, at room temperature

2 teaspoons finely grated lime zest

397-g/14-oz. can sweetened condensed milk

150 ml/⅔ cup freshly squeezed lime juice (from about 6 limes)

200 ml/¾ cup double/heavy cream

1 tablespoon icing/confectioners' sugar

lime slices, to decorate

a 23-cm/9-inch tart pan, 2.5 cm/1 inch deep

SERVES 8

MANGO CURD PAVLOVA PIE

This is an outrage of a pie! Clouds of gooey pavlova meringue float on top of a luscious filling of fresh mango curd. Lime is the natural partner to mango, enhancing the wonderful exotic taste. If really good ripe mangoes are difficult to find, try using canned Alphonso mango purée – they have the best flavour and can be found at Asian stores.

1 quantity Rich Shortcrust
Pastry (see page 24)

1 egg, beaten

FOR THE MANGO CURD FILLING:

500 g/1 lb. 2 oz. ripe mango flesh
(about 2 large mangoes), chopped

125 g/⅔ cup caster/granulated
sugar

finely grated zest and freshly
squeezed juice of 2 limes

3 whole eggs, plus 4 egg yolks

FOR THE PAVLOVA TOPPING :

4 egg whites

a pinch of salt

225 g/1 cup plus 2 tablespoons
caster/superfine sugar

1 teaspoon cornflour/cornstarch

1 teaspoon pure vanilla extract

1 teaspoon vinegar

a 23-cm/9-inch loose-based tart pan

SERVES 6

Preheat the oven to 190°F (375°C) Gas 5.

Roll out the pastry on a lightly-floured surface and use to line the pie plate. Prick the base of the pastry with a fork, line with baking parchment or kitchen foil, then fill with baking beans and bake blind for 15 minutes. Remove from the oven and brush the whole inside of the tart with beaten egg, then return to the oven for 5 minutes until the egg glaze has cooked. Brush and bake again if necessary, then leave to cool.

For the filling, blend the mango flesh, sugar and lime zest and juice in a food processor until smooth, scraping down the side occasionally. Add the whole eggs and egg yolks and process for a few seconds more until mixed. Strain the curd mixture through a coarse sieve/strainer into the pie crust and spread out evenly.

Reduce the oven temperature to 140°C (275°F) Gas 1.

For the topping, whisk the egg whites and salt with an electric hand-whisk until very stiff. Gradually whisk in the sugar, one large spoonful at a time, making sure the meringue is really 'bouncily' stiff before adding the next spoonful. Whisk in the cornflour/cornstarch, vanilla and vinegar. Spoon evenly over the pie, ensuring that you seal the edges with meringue. Pile this as high as you can!

Bake for about 45 minutes until the meringue is just turning palest brown. Remove the pie from the oven, cool for a few minutes then serve warm (the filling may still be a bit soft) or leave to cool completely (the filling will be firm) and serve cold.

INDEX

ACKNOWLEDGMENTS

I would like to thank the lovely Julia Charles for thinking about me in the first place and suggesting that I write this book – right up my street Julia, thanks! I must also thank my editor Rebecca Woods for keeping me on track through some tricky times in such a sweet and understanding way, and for her patience and thorough checking of my sporadic copy – you have worked miracles! My long-time colleague and friend Steve Painter photographed, styled and designed this book so beautifully, with such attention to detail, that I was speechless when the page proofs arrived. Together, we discussed the look of the book and certain essential details by phone and I sent him a few treasured pie props, and he did all the rest – just beautifully. But where did the actual pies come from? They came from the talented hands and limitless imagination of Lucy McKelvie – Lucy you made them just as I would have… and with such cleverness and care. I know how long these things take to make and just don't know how you did it in the time! You and Steve have created some truly magical shots.